The LEXIS® Companion

The LEXIS®
Companion

·············

A Complete Guide to Effective Searching

Jean Sinclair McKnight

Addison-Wesley Publishing Company

Reading, Massachusetts   Menlo Park, California   New York
Don Mills, Ontario   Wokingham, England   Amsterdam
Bonn   Sydney   Singapore   Tokyo   Madrid   San Juan
Paris   Seoul   Milan   Mexico City   Taipei

Many of the designations used by manufacturers and sellers to distinguish their products are claimed as trademarks. Where those designations appear in this book, and Addison-Wesley was aware of a trademark claim, the designations have been printed with initial capital letters or all capital letters.

The author and publisher have taken care in preparation of this book, but make no expressed or implied warranty of any kind and assume no responsibility for errors or omissions. No liability is assumed for incidental or consequential damages in connection with or arising out of the use of the information or programs contained herein.

Library of Congress Cataloging-in-Publication Data

McKnight, Jean Sinclair.
   The LEXIS companion : a complete guide to effective searching /
   Jean Sinclair McKnight.
      p.   cm.
   Includes index.
   ISBN 0-201-48335-1
   1. LEXIS (Information retrieval system)   2. Legal research—United
   States—Data processing.   I. Title.
   KF242.A1M35   1995
   025.06'34—dc20   95-22398
                                                                CIP

Sponsoring Editor: Claire Horne
Project Manager: John Fuller
Production Coordinator: Ellen Savett
Cover design: Andrew Newman
Text design: Joyce C. Weston
Set in 11-point Minion by A & B Typesetters, Inc.

1 2 3 4 5 6 7 8 9 -DOH- 9998979695
First printing, August 1995

Addison-Wesley books are available for bulk purchases by corporations, institutions, and other organizations. For more information please contact the Corporate, Government, and Special Sales Department at (800) 238-9682.

For my father, Michael Loy Sinclair,
who finally convinced me that computers don't bite;

and my sons, Forrest and Will;

and my beloved husband, Ed.
Thank you for everything.

CONTENTS

1

Introduction

THIS CHAPTER COVERS:

What's a LEXIS?

What is full-text searching, and what good is it?

The commands shown in this book

Top ten reasons to use LEXIS

The limitations of LEXIS

What you need to access LEXIS

A quick look at the big picture

A sample research session

What's a LEXIS?

LEXIS IS a tremendous database of legal research materials, including federal and state statutes and cases, secondary sources, citators, and much more. It is located in Dayton, Ohio, and can be accessed through phone lines by subscribers using an appropriately equipped personal computer. LEXIS has a non-legal counterpart, NEXIS, which can be accessed by LEXIS subscribers and contains a fantastic array of news and business sources (from the *New York Times* and transcripts of National Public Radio broadcasts to *Aerospace Daily* and the *Boomer Times,* an entire periodical devoted to the lifestyle and spending habits of baby boomers). You can read the full text of an opinion hours after it is handed down by the Supreme Court and see which blender *Consumer Reports* says is best without ever leaving

1

your chair. It's one-stop shopping for the information age, and once you learn your way around, you'll wonder how you ever got along without it. Recognizing that you are probably eager to get started but may not have enough twinkies and chips on hand to make it through this manual in one sitting, I have included a sample research session at the end of this chapter, with copious references to relevant chapters at each step, so that you can read the whole book on a crisis-by-crisis basis instead of straight through, if that's your preference.

What Is Full-Text Searching, and What Good Is It?

Perhaps even more valuable to researchers than the sheer volume of materials LEXIS offers is the fact that all those materials are "full-text searchable." This means that a researcher can find *any* word or phrase in *any* document on the system simply by "asking" for it. Unlike traditional materials that are accessible only through indexes, LEXIS materials are accessible through any word or phrase in their text. This means the researcher is no longer at the mercy of an indexer who decides what is important and what heading to list it under. The downside of this is that a researcher who doesn't know quite what he or she is looking for or what is out there doesn't get the benefit of the clues in an index. With an index you know what your choices are, even though you may wish there were more of them. With full-text searching you have no end of choices, but no built-in clues as to where to start. Pick your poison.

The Commands Shown in This Book

There are several different versions of LEXIS software (various versions for DOS, Windows, Macintosh), which offer various ways to enter commands and different screen formats. The commands and instructions given in this book are typed or "dot" commands (one- or two-letter abbreviations, often begun with a period or "dot"), which will work with a version of LEXIS research software. However, you may find it easier to use one of the special methods available with your software to give commands. For example, if you have Windows, you can click on the commands that appear on the screen, or with other versions you can use function keys designated for various commands. It is still worth your while (and necessary for optimum searching capabilities) to learn the typed dot commands so you will recognize all the possible commands, and so you will have the advantage of being able to use those that do not appear on a given Windows screen (many useful commands will not be shown on the screens for lack of space) or that do not have a designated function key. Further, the typed dot commands allow you to enter commands quickly without moving your fingers from the letter keys, to take advantage of the SHORT CUT feature (see Chapter 8), and to move easily from one LEXIS terminal or software package to another without learning a new research style.

Top Ten Reasons to Use LEXIS

LEXIS gives you

1. Access to a fantastic array of sources. LEXIS gives you access to more legal information than you could possibly hope to acquire and maintain in any library (nearly 200 million documents).

2. Unique searching capabilities. It gives you access to the full text of these materials and lets you search for any term or phrase, anywhere, rather than the terms an indexer selected.

3. Currentness unmatched by print. Many cases appear on-line within hours of being handed down. There are no mailing, printing, or receiving lag times.

4. Twenty-four-hour access. All the information in LEXIS is available 24 hours a day (except 2 A.M. to 10 A.M. Sunday), every day except Christmas.

5. *It is never missing from the shelf when you need it.*

6. *It can save you library space and maintenance.* LEXIS doesn't take up shelf space or require upkeep (except in the form of cash, which it devours in great quantities). LEXIS requires no filing, no shelving, no ordering and processing, no binding, and no circulation records.

7. *It can save you time.* Most research can be done more quickly on-line than in print. There is no need to travel to a library or wait for books to be returned, ordered, or borrowed from another library. Even when the library has everything you need, there is no hunting for the books you need, searching indexes and finding aids for the documents you want, or skimming through page after page looking for a mention of a specific term or phrase you can now find with a few keystrokes.

8. *It can save you money.* LEXIS is extremely expensive, but it can save you money if you use it well: money for acquiring and maintaining materials you rarely use but must have occasionally, money for document-delivery services, money for manual cite-checks, and, as noted in item 7, money for your time.

9. *It can save you clients.* LEXIS gives you the information and time you need to answer your clients' questions and win their cases.

10. *Free T-shirts, cups, clocks, egg-timers...* You name it, LEXIS will put their name on it and give it away eventually. Few material goods are as likely to win friends and influence people as the official LEXIS one-end-is-a-pen-and-the-other-is-a-highlighter, and your odds of receiving one go up appreciably (and inexplicably—after all, they already have *your* money) when you become a LEXIS subscriber.

The Limitations of LEXIS

LEXIS can't tell you what you're looking for if you don't know. It is stunningly expensive, especially if you don't use it efficiently. It doesn't contain all sources in the known universe. You can't take notes in its margins or browse through it repeatedly without extra charges, and it doesn't tastefully decorate your office the way all those shelves of matching law books do. LEXIS has no index, which makes it very hard to know what you might be missing or where to start looking. It cannot absolve you of malpractice. Researching on-line is not enough—you have to research *well*. Thorough research in books is all that is required of lawyers at this time, although the expectation that a lawyer should use an on-line legal research service may develop as such services become more widely used (see Simon Chester, *Electronic Malpractice: Does reasonable competence require computer research?*, Law Practice Management, Nov/Dec 1991, at 23).

What You Need to Access LEXIS

If you are interested in getting LEXIS and want to know exactly what is involved, here is what you need to get access to LEXIS:

1. A computer. You need *either* an IBM PC-compatible with DOS 3.0 or higher, 4 MB of available disk space, 512K (minimum) of RAM, of which at least 400K is available;

    or an IBM PC-compatible with Windows 3.0 or higher, at least 4 MB of available disk space, 4 MB of RAM, and a 3.5-inch floppy drive (a mouse is extremely helpful with this setup, but not absolutely necessary);

    or an Apple Macintosh with at least 512K of memory and system 4.1 (minimum)/finder 5.5 (minimum) software.

2. A modem and phone line. These should be Hayes-compatible. Any modem 1200 baud or faster will work, but if you have a choice, get the fastest modem you can—it will quickly pay for itself in saved time and connect charges.

3. A printer. A printer is not strictly necessary, but it *is* a big help and in most cases is a money saver. Even access to one that is not attached to your computer is a big help, as you can download the information you need to a disk and carry the disk to the printer.

4. A subscription. If you looked into LEXIS years ago and decided you couldn't afford it, look again. There are several new pricing options, and some offer vastly improved deals for small firms or solo practitioners. See Chapter 12, and ask the LEXIS salespeople if there is anything new.

5. Research software and a password supplied by LEXIS with your subscription.

If any or all of this confuses you, or you don't already have the appropriate hardware lying around the house, fear not. LEXIS will be all too happy to help you get set up so you can start paying LEXIS bills regularly. Just call 1-800-543-6862, and your off-line days will soon be an empty, distant memory.

A Quick Look at the Big Picture

It is easy to feel lost and disoriented when you first start using LEXIS. It may help to realize how reassuringly few options you really have (at least reassuringly few basic procedures—OK, sure, you still have bazillions of possible refinements, but that's what the rest of this book is for).

A LEXIS research session always begins with signing on and ends with signing off. In between, you basically have three options:

Option 1: You can retrieve a document by citation, using LEXSEE or LEXSTAT.

Option 2: You can choose a library and file and search for documents using terms and connectors (Boolean searching) or natural language.

Option 3: You can use a citator (Shepard's, Auto-Cite, or LEXSEE).

You can do any or all of these things, as many times as you want and in any order, until you are bankrupt. Once you've found something, you can browse through it, print, or save your results on a disk, and/or have your search updated automatically at specified intervals. Then you can do it all again or sign off and wait for the bill to come in the mail.

To give you a little more idea of how you do all these things and what it looks like on the screen when you do, I have included the following sample research session, showing a good representative sample of basic searches. A really detailed sample search session could easily fill hundreds of pages, but that wouldn't be much fun for either of us, so here goes the short version.

A Sample Research Session

This sample research session is intended to give you an idea of what is out there. It is sort of a guided tour of LEXIS—just enough to show you the lay of the land.

1. System requirements. To use LEXIS you must have a computer with a modem and LEXIS research software installed on it. LEXIS is eager to get you past this first hurdle so they can start taking your money—so if you want to open an account or need technical support, don't be shy—call 1-800-543-6862.

2. First step. Turn the computer on and start the LEXIS research software. Follow the instructions with your software to turn the LEXIS research software on (usually typing `LEXIS` at the C prompt and pressing Enter will do it).

3. Enter your password when prompted to do so. Type in your LEXIS password and press Enter. Just start typing; the cursor should already be in the correct location at the top left corner of the screen. Your password may not be displayed, but if you enter it correctly you should see a screen like Figure 1.1. If you are thinking "Password?

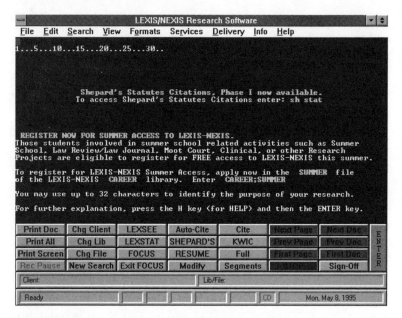

Figure 1.1

What password?"—or if the computer doesn't accept the password you have—talk to your account representative.

4. Enter your client identification information. Or not. Enter the identifier of your choice (up to 32 characters) on that unfathomable 1 ... 5 ... 10 ... etc. line (see Figure 1.1), or press Enter to skip over this step. Remember that if you don't identify the client you are researching for now, you can't bill the client later, and you or someone who can fire you on the slightest provocation will be left holding the bill.

5. The Library menu (see Figure 1.2). From this point you can do lots of different things. You could use a service to retrieve a document by citation, use a citator, or choose a library and file and search using natural language or terms and connectors. You can do any or all of these things in any order you like. For illustrative purposes in this sample search I arbitrarily use a service (LEXSTAT) first.

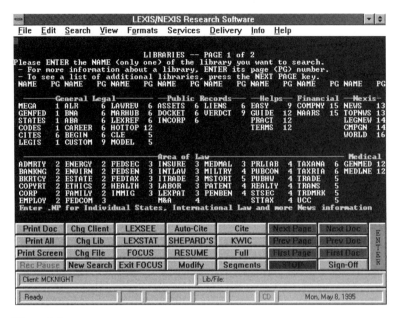

Figure 1.2

6. *Retrieve a statute by citation: LEXSTAT.* To use LEXSTAT to re-trieve a statute by its citation simply type LEXSTAT and the citation and press the Enter or Return key on your keyboard. For example, to retrieve 1 US 101 just type LEXSTAT 1 US 101 at the top of the Library menu screen and press Enter. The first screen of the case will be displayed.

Having retrieved a document, you can page through the full text of it by pushing (or clicking on) Enter or Page Down (see Chapter 4 for more complete information on viewing documents). You can print out a screen or the whole document.

7. *FOCUS.* If you want to find a particular term or terms in the doc-ument you have retrieved, you use FOCUS; you type in what you are looking for and FOCUS takes you straight to the place(s) it appears in your document. Say you have just retrieved a regulation on safe

well installation, and you want to skip right to the part that talks about whether you can use chlorine bleach to disinfect the water. Instead of reading the whole statute, which might be 50 pages long, type `focus chlorine bleach` and press Enter, and bingo, the first screen where "chlorine bleach" appears in the document is displayed, with the terms you searched for (chlorine bleach) highlighted. Press Enter again and the next screen where "chlorine bleach" appears is displayed, and so on. To exit FOCUS and get on with your searching or printing or life, enter `.ef`.

8. Receive a case by citation: LEXSEE. LEXSEE works just like LEXSTAT for non-statutory materials. You can retrieve any state or federal case using LEXSEE, as well as ALR annotations, federal regulations, IRS documents, many law review articles, and other documents (see Chapter 3 for details on LEXSEE and LEXSTAT coverage and use). To search for a case or other non-statutory document (eligible publications are listed in Appendix D), type `LEXSEE` and the citation (in the form listed in Appendix D for that publication) and enter. Voila, if your cite is in the correct form and you've been living right, you will see the first screen of your document.

You can use LEXSEE or LEXSTAT to retrieve as many documents as you like without returning to the library menu each time; just keep typing in citations. To search by anything other than citation, you must return to the library menu by entering `.es`.

9. Choose a library and file to search. You save on-line time and money by consulting a database list before you sign on, so that you know what library and file best suits your needs (see Chapter 2). After you select a library and enter its identifier (the abbreviated library name, listed on the menu screen—see Figure 1.2), the File menu will be displayed (see Figure 1.3). Which File menu you see depends on which library you selected. Let's say we selected the GEN-FED library. The menu of files available in the GENFED library will then appear (see Figure 1.3).

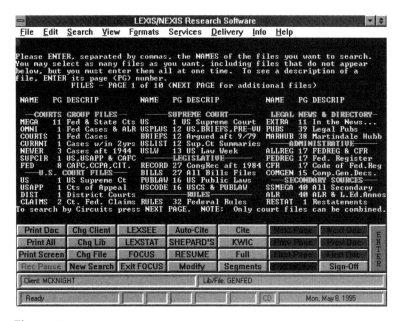

Figure 1.3

10. Enter your query. After selecting an appropriate file (let's say Courts) by entering its identifier, the system will prompt you to enter your query (search). See Figure 1.4. You can enter a query using terms and connectors or natural language (see Chapters 3 and 4). To search for cases about whether Vietnamese pot-bellied pigs are considered livestock for zoning purposes using terms and connectors you might enter `vietnamese pot-bellied pigs w/25 livestock and zoning`. You would retrieve one case, which is right on point.

11. Freestyle Searching. To search for the same sort of case using Freestyle, you first enter `.fr` to switch to Freestyle mode. Then you might enter `Are vietnamese pot-bellied pigs considered livestock?` You get 25 cases (you always get just the first 25 cases with Freestyle unless you tell it differently). Six of those are relevant. The others are *way* off in left field.

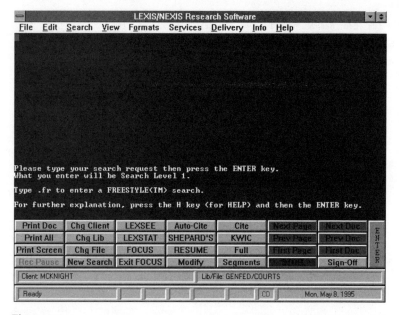

Figure 1.4

12. Segment searching. You can limit your search to particular parts of documents (titles only, or the part that identifies judges or counsel, for example—see Chapter 4). This enables you to do many kinds of searches that are not possible (or at least not practical) in books. For example, you can search for all the opinions written by a particular judge (`writtenby(thomas)`), or all the cases argued by your cousin Vinnie (`counsel (Vincenzio and Barducci)`), or a law review article for which you can remember only a partial title (`title(hand that rocked the cradle)`). You can also use segments, once you have retrieved a document, to go quickly to a particular part of that document. If, for example, you want to skip directly to the dissent in a case you have just received, you can enter `.se` to see a list of available segments (see Figure 1.5), and then enter `dissent`. The first page of the dissent will be displayed. You can then restore the rest of the text of the document to view by entering `.fu` for full.

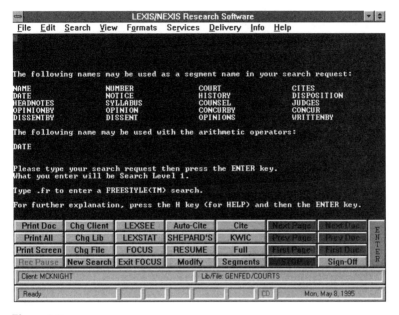

Figure 1.5

13. *Date restriction.* You can restrict your search to documents dated on, after, or before a particular date or during or outside a range of dates. We could search for cases involving Vietnamese pot-bellied pigs since 1992 (`Vietnamese pot-bellied pig and date aft 1991`). See Chapter 4.

14. *Display format.* Once you have entered your query, the number of documents retrieved will be displayed and you will be prompted to select a display format (see Figure 1.6). You can choose to see the full text of the documents (`FULL`), excerpts containing your search terms (`KWIC`), or just the documents' citations (`CITE`). See Chapter 5.

15. *Browsing through retrieved documents.* You can go to the next page of your document by pressing Enter or Next Page. There are previous page (`.pp`), previous document (`.pd`), first page (`.fp`),

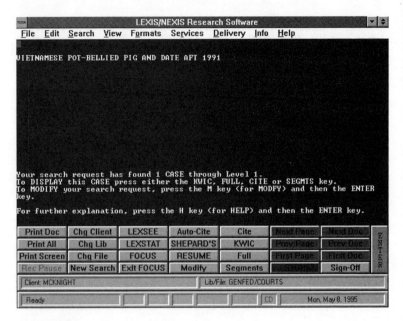

Figure 1.6

and first document (`.fd`) commands available for your browsing convenience (see Chapter 5). You can locate specific terms within retrieved documents using FOCUS. See Chapter 5.

16. Modifying a search. If you are not satisfied with your search results, you can modify your search (see Chapter 4). For example, we could modify the Vietnamese pot-bellied pig search to include dog-bite cases. The system would then display a different level of search results, which can be browsed though like the first. You can move to a different level's results by entering `dl#`, where # is the number of the level you want to review.

17. Printing. You can print a screen you are viewing (`.sp`), select one (`.pr`) or more (`.pa`) documents to print, or save to a disk after you sign off. You will be prompted to select a printer or disk drive and confirm your print request. If you choose Print All, you can select all or some of the documents retrieved by your current search to print. See Chapter 7.

18. LINK. While you are viewing a document you may want also to view another document cited there. To do this, you can use the LINK feature or the LEXSEE or LEXSTAT services without losing your place. For example, from the screen shown in Figure 1.7, you could retrieve the case cited beside the < = 1 > link marker by typing = 1 and Enter. If a cited document has no link marker (the < = # >), you can use LEXSEE or LEXSTAT to view it (see Chapter 3). Whichever method you use to retrieve the cited document, you can browse or print it to your heart's content and then enter resume to return to your original document.

19. Shepard's Citations. LEXIS offers several citators (see Chapter 6). Once you have retrieved a document by any method, you can

Figure 1.7

Shepardize it simply by typing . sh. This will get you a Shepard's display like Figure 1.8 (see Chapter 6 for more information). To Shepardize a case you are not viewing, type . sh and the citation and Enter. You can jump to the full text of any citing case on the Shepard's screen by entering or clicking on its number (see Chapter 6).

20. Auto-Cite. In addition to the old reliable Shepard's citator, you can use Auto-Cite to see if your case is in correct *Bluebook* form and whether anything has happened to affect its precedential value. As you can with Shepard's, you can access it two ways—by entering . ac while viewing the case, or by typing . ac and the citation and Enter. Auto-Citing the same case gets us a display like Figure 1.9 (see Chapter 6 for further explanation of Auto-Cite).

21. LEXIS as a citator. To use LEXIS as a citator, you search for a cited document as a search query in a library and file. For example, you

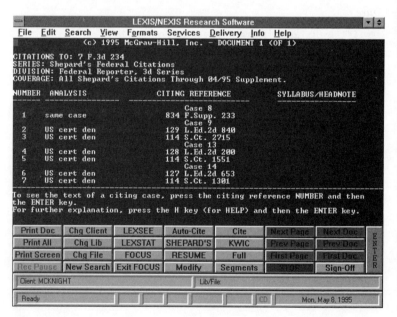

Figure 1.8

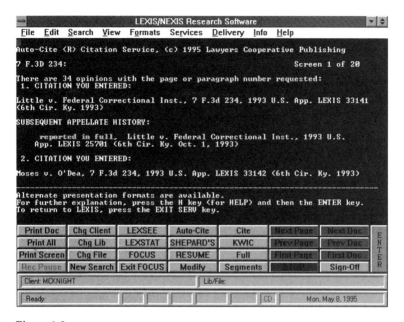

Figure 1.9

might search for an unpublished opinion, since only published opinions are covered by Shepard's. You might also search for an article by title, to find cases that have cited it. You can search for citations to any document, using any identifying information you choose, unlike the other citators, which cover only cases and selected law reviews. Using LEXIS as a citator allows you to retrieve citations to some documents not covered by Shepard's or Auto-Cite and to find the very most recent citing materials (it takes weeks if not months for a document to find its way into Shepard's, since an editorial process is involved). See Chapter 6.

22. LEXCITE. LEXCITE is the automated form of LEXIS as a citator, and it gives the most current citing references without any editorial interpretation. You get the citing references themselves and have to read them to decide what their importance is. Unlike using Shepard's and Auto-Cite, with LEXCITE you have to select a library and file for the citing references to be drawn from before you use LEXSTAT. Then you enter LEXSTAT and the citation to which you want to find references. You get documents that cite yours, full-text and unadorned. You can browse through them as you can any other search results, using KWIC (to go right to the citation in the text), FOCUS, and so on. See Chapter 6.

23. *Advance Legislative Services.* You can update statutes using an advance legislative service or even track pending legislation that might affect a statute. See Chapter 6.

24. *ECLIPSE.* To have the system update a search for you on a daily, weekly, or monthly basis, you can request an ECLIPSE search (see Chapter 8).

25. *Changing your library or file.* You can change your library and/or file and do a new search at any time by entering .cl to change library or .cf to change files.

26. *NEXIS.* You can do a lot more than search for cases and statutes on LEXIS. NEXIS non-legal but law-related databases offer just about every kind of information you might need in the fact-gathering portion of litigation—and for the non-law portion of your existence.

To access NEXIS, you choose NEXIS from the LEXIS library menu and then select a NEXIS file in which to search. You can search major newspapers, magazines, and transcripts of broadcast news programs. See Chapter 10.

27. *The BEGIN library.* You can search some secondary sources, including ALR (the equivalent of Cliff Notes for lawyers—a great time and mistake saver) and the Restatements using the BEGIN library. The LINK feature is available in the Restatement database. This feature allows you to move quickly to a particular topic of the Restatement, with all updates appended. If you have ever used a paper copy of a Restatement, you know what a big advantage this is.

28. The EASY Library. If it all seems too overwhelming, you can have your choices all laid out for you by using the EASY library (see Chapter 2) as long as the files you need to search are included in it. It offers step-by-step prompts to guide you through most basic searches. The downside of the EASY library is that it is slow and expensive and does not allow you access to all LEXIS/NEXIS files.

29. Cost. When your research is done, you can see how much you have spent by using the Cost command (see Chapter 12). This is not an exercise for the faint of heart.

30. Time. The Time command tells you how long you've been on-line. See Chapter 12.

31. SHORT CUT. The SHORT CUT feature allows you to "stack" your commands to save time. For example, you can enter your password, client ID, library and file selection, search query, and display format choice all at once instead of entering commands on six different screens. See Chapter 8.

32. LOG. Type .keep to store the results of a search on-line until 2 A.M. Eastern time. Then type .log to retrieve those results and browse or modify them without additional search charges. See Chapter 8.

33. The CAREER library. You can search for employer information and print a mailing list for your résumé in minutes. See Chapter 9.

34. CUSTOM. When you've searched to your heart's content, you might consider LEXIS's Private Database Services, which allow you to create a litigation support library of your own briefs, forms, and memos. The CUSTOM library is basically an advertisement for this service. CUSTOM is a free library—there are no connect, telecommunications, search, or print charges, so you might want to take a look. For more information on LEXIS's Private Database Services, call 1-800-362-8163.

35. SIGNING OFF. To sign off, type `. so` and press Enter. You will be asked whether you want to save your research until 2 A.M. or not. You might as well, since it is free and just as easy as not saving it. It can save you a lot of trouble and even some money when that cup of coffee kicks in later and you want to take another run at the search you gave up on, or when there is a printing problem and you need to re-enter your print request.

2

Choosing a Library and File

THIS CHAPTER COVERS:

How to open a library and file

Library and file selection

Sources of information about libraries and files

Combining files

Avoiding libraries and files when possible

The Easy Search library

T HE LEXIS database contains more than 188 million documents. To make the database more manageable, it is separated into libraries and files. If you think of the LEXIS database as a warehouse full of filing cabinets, libraries are analogous to single drawers in the filing cabinets. Each *library* is composed of several *files*, and each file is full of documents (a document is a single case, statute, article, annotation, and so on). To search for documents, you must select a library and file. The exception to this rule is that if you have a citation to a specific document, you can use a service (LEXSEE, LEXSTAT, LINK, Shepard's, or Auto-Cite, all described in detail in later chapters) to retrieve the document or its citator table for you while you are looking in another library and file or while you are still on a library or file menu screen.

How to Open a Library and File

The first screen you see after you have logged on and entered your client identification information is the Library menu (see Figure 2.1). There are two library menu screens full of libraries to choose from (to see the second screen, as shown in Figure 2.2, press Enter or Page Down).

To open a library, enter its identifier. For example, to choose the Alabama library, type `ala` and press Enter. Each library is composed of files. There are more than 3,900 files in the LEXIS/NEXIS database. After you choose a library, a file menu consisting only of the files available in the library you just chose will be displayed. It may be several screens long. You can move from one screen to another using the Page Down and Page Up keys. Open a file by typing its identifier and pressing Enter.

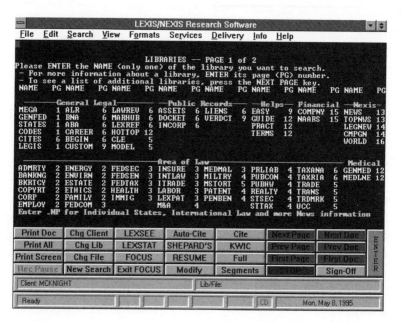

Figure 2.1

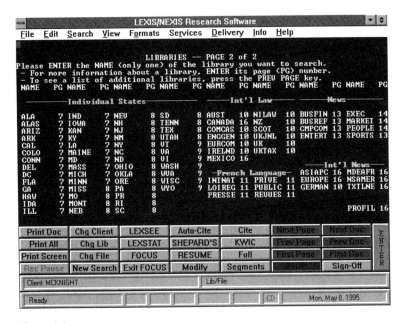

Figure 2.2

Only after you choose a library and file can you enter your search query. Formulating and entering a search query is covered in Chapter 3.

Library and File Selection

Opening a file is easy. Choosing the right file is a little more tricky (not much) and completely crucial to successful and efficient research. What library and file you choose determines what documents you can retrieve and how much you will pay for your search. First and foremost, you must choose a library and file that contains the information you want. If you don't bother to identify the appropriate library and file for your research needs carefully, you *will* eventually miss a pivotal document. Attorneys might as well have the backs of their suits imprinted with the words "Please sue me" as be careless on this point. ("Well, your honor, it is true that I did not find the controlling law, but you see, there were all these little library and file thingies to choose from, and I was really in a hurry, and it just seemed like so much *trouble* to check to see which one covered the jurisdiction and time frames I needed. . . .")

$ Another reason to select libraries and files carefully is money (funny how this just keeps coming up). You can save time and money by choosing the smallest, cheapest database that has what you need in it. For example, suppose you want to retrieve all recent Vermont cases dealing with food processors. You could choose the MEGA library and the MEGA file. This file has all federal and state cases in it, so it contains any available Vermont cases. A single search in this library and file would cost approximately $95 and retrieve 392 documents, only 2 of which are Vermont state cases. Alternatively, you could search in the Vermont library case file for approximately $24. You would retrieve the same Vermont cases, without all the other cases to wade through, and save $71 on a single search, not counting wasted time spent picking out Vermont cases from all the others. The trick, then, is to be able to identify the smallest, least expensive library and file that suits your needs. To do this, you need more information about the libraries and files than is available on the menu screens, at least until you are familiar with the alternatives.

Sources of Information about Libraries and Files

LEXIS/NEXIS provides several printed guides to library and file contents and pricing. They are:

- The *LEXIS/NEXIS Library Contents and Alphabetical List*, which lists library and file names, their abbreviations, and major coverage dates

- The *LEXIS Product Guide*, which lists all the libraries and files and provides detailed descriptions of their coverage, including what segments they contain (see Chapter 4 for an explanation of what segments are and what you can do with them)

♦ The LEXIS price list, which (surprise, surprise) lists prices for libraries and files

All of these printed sources are updated "periodically," which means when there are enough changes to make it worth the LEXIS staff's while *and* they get around to it. There are several on-line sources of information about libraries and files that are kept more current.

Menu Screens

Most obvious are the menu screens. Beside each library and file there is a number that you can enter in order to see a description of the library or file contents. You can then press Page Up or Down to see adjacent descriptions, or enter `.fp` to see the first page of the library descriptions. Enter `.cl` (for choose library) or `.cf` (for choose file) to return to a library or file menu. Choosing a library and file from the menu screens is tempting because it is so easy (you never forget where you left them, for one thing), but it doesn't give you much information on which to base your decision.

The GUIDE Library

The GUIDE library offers more detailed content descriptions and is free. You can select the GUIDE library from the library menu screen, or once you have selected another library, you can view descriptions of the files therein by using the GUIDE file. GUIDE gives library and file names, publications covered, coverage dates, other libraries and files in which the described file is included, what kind of documents are available in the file, and samples of the kinds of search requests that work in the file. To open the GUIDE library, enter `guide` on a library or file menu screen. If you enter GUIDE on a library screen, you get a screen like Figure 2.3 and can choose to access any GUIDE file.

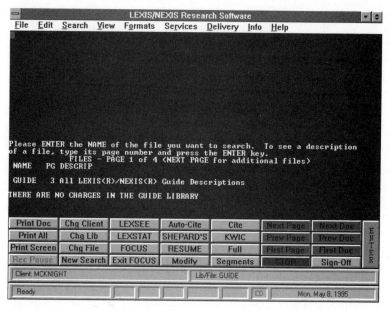

Figure 2.3

If you enter GUIDE on a file screen, you have access only to the GUIDE for files available in the library you have already selected (you have already selected a library or you wouldn't be on a file menu screen; if you don't remember selecting one or want to choose a different one, type .cl to return to the first library screen).

The Contents File: To see the table of contents for the GUIDE library, type CNTNTS on the GUIDE screen (see Figure 2.3). The first item on the menu screen that will appear includes an alphabetical list of publications and sources available on LEXIS/NEXIS, with coverage dates (see Figure 2.4).

You can follow the directions on the screen to go to the first letter of the item in question and scroll through the list using the Page Down and Page Up keys or type .ns and do a search using terms and connectors (see Chapter 3). For example, if you want to find a library and file that has articles from the *New York Times*, you could type New York Times and press Enter, and you would be re-

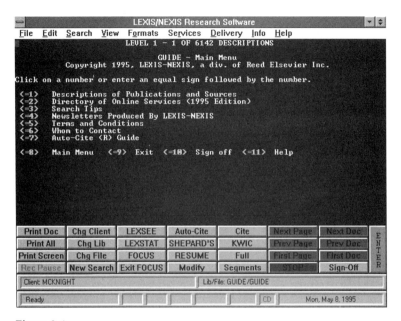

Figure 2.4

warded with a list of descriptions of databases containing articles from the *New York Times*.

The DEBUT Screen

A third on-line source of information about libraries and files is the DEBUT screen, the screen that appears when you first sign on and shows the very latest ways LEXIS has devised to part you from your money. A DEBUT screen looks something like Figure 2.5.

Combining Files

In most libraries it is possible to search more than one file at the same time, as long as the files are in the same library. Simply enter the file identifiers, separated by commas, at the top of the file menu screen. This is called *custom file selection*. The cost of custom file se-

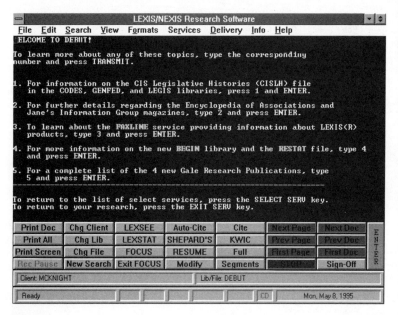

Figure 2.5

lection varies from library to library. Within a library, the cost stays the same whether you combine two, three, or more files.

$ It is usually cheaper to search files separately unless you are going to use the same search in more than two files from the same library. Even with three files it is important to check current prices to see if custom file selection offers a savings.

Avoiding Libraries and Files When Possible

$ Use a service instead (LEXSEE, LEXSTAT, or LINK) whenever you can (when you have a citation). The services cost $4 to $5 a search, while searching a library and file costs $24 to $95. Thus, each time you use LEXSEE to retrieve a case instead of searching a library and file for it, you save between $19 and $91 (plus you save a little time). Similarly, don't pull up a case in a library and file ($24 to $95) to Shepardize or Auto-Cite it (see Chapter 6) when you can just Shepardize or Auto-Cite its citation ($4 to $5) instead.

The Easy Search Library

For novice researchers LEXIS offers the Easy Search library, which offers step-by-step menu access to commonly used materials. You can use this easily, even if you've never done anything with a computer before. Select EASY from the library menu and follow the prompts on your screen.

So why use anything else? Many materials are not accessible through this library. Furthermore it is slow, tedious, and limiting compared to the wonders of Boolean and Freestyle searching, which are about to be revealed to you in the next chapter!

CHAPTER 2.   QUICK REFERENCE PAGE

.cl = Change Library
.cf = Change File

Choose the GUIDE library to see library and file contents descriptions.

Choose the CNTNTS file (in the GUIDE library) to see a list of publications available on LEXIS.

Remember: you don't have to choose a library or file at all to use LEXSEE, LEXSTAT, Shepard's, or Auto-Cite.

3

Basics of Document Retrieval

THIS CHAPTER COVERS:

Entering and editing commands

Retrieving documents by citation

(LEXSEE and LEXSTAT)

Searching with terms and connectors

Natural language searching (Freestyle)

THIS CHAPTER covers basic searching techniques: entering and editing searches and commands, retrieving documents by citation, and searching with terms and connectors or with natural language. Before you can do any of these things you have to sign on (see Chapter 1). You also need to choose a library and file before searching with terms and connectors or with natural language (see Chapter 2).

Entering and Editing Commands

LEXIS commands are typed near the top of the screen. The cursor starts out in the right place so you can usually just start typing; if it has strayed away, you can coax it back to the top of the screen using the arrow keys.

Enter = Transmit = Return

Each time you type a command you must press Enter (marked Transmit or Return on some keyboards, and always referred to as

Transmit in LEXIS documentation and on-screen instructions) to send it to LEXIS.

Look before You Enter

$ After you type a command, you should always proofread it before entering it, since mistakes can be quite costly (a new search costs between $24 and $95). If you make a mistake, you can use the arrow keys to move the cursor back to it and type over it.

Typeover versus Insert Mode

LEXIS operates by default in typeover mode, which means that if you put the cursor on an existing character and type a new one, the new character will replace the old one. You may find this irritating if you are used to working with a word processor that works in insert mode instead. You can convert LEXIS to your way of doing things by pressing the Insert key on your keyboard.

Correcting Errors

$ Once you have moved your cursor backwards to correct an error in your command, be sure to move it to the end of the command before entering it, or the part of the command after the cursor will be lost. This sort of error is expensive and easily avoidable. Get in the habit of always, always proofreading your command and making sure the cursor is at the end of it before pressing Enter.

Capitalization

LEXIS doesn't differentiate between upper- and lowercase letters, either in what you type in or in what it retrieves, unless you instruct it to using the CAPS, ALLCAPS, and NOCAPS commands. Having LEXIS ignore the case of what you type is usually an advantage, since it gives you one less way to make a mistake. If you always lose your place and blunder around the keyboard for a moment after reaching for the Shift key to capitalize something, you will especially enjoy this freedom. Once in a long while, however, you'll have a special need to have LEXIS differentiate between upper- and lowercase letters. CAPS retrieves words with at least one capital letter. ALLCAPS retrieves only words in all capitals, and NOCAPS retrieves words with no capital letters. To use these commands, you type them in front of the word you want them to affect, like so: CAPS(Kleenex).

Clicking for Windows and Mac Users

If you are using Windows or Macintosh software, you can often point and click on the command you want. If the command you want is not shown in one of the buttons on the screen, it may be available from one of the pull-down menus (see Figure 3.1). You can use a keyboard command if you prefer, and sometimes you may want to since you may not know exactly where to find a command on the screen.

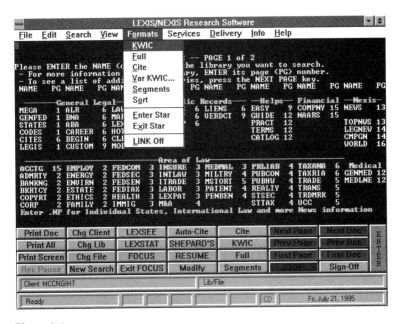

Figure 3.1

■ **RULES TO TYPE BY**

1. Always proofread your command before transmitting (entering) it.
2. Always move your cursor to the end of the command before pressing Enter or Transmit.
3. Capitalization or lack thereof doesn't matter. ■

LEXIS Keys

The keys you use to enter commands vary depending on the kind of operating system you are using: DOS, Windows, or Macintosh. DOS uses function keys and a template, which comes with your research software. Windows and Macintosh use on-screen prompts (see Figure 3.1). With any of these systems you can use dot and shortcut commands: abbreviations of commands that you keyboard in. To enter one of these commands, you type it in and press the Enter key. It is a very good idea to learn to use these commands regardless of the operating system you are using, since they enable you to use several money- and time-saving strategies not otherwise available to you (see Chapter 8). Because these commands are applicable to each system and because of the advantages they offer (primarily the SHORT CUT feature, described in Chapter 8), I have chosen to give directions throughout this book using dot (so called because they begin with a "dot," or period) and other abbreviated commands. Those commands are as follows:

```
.ns = NEW SEARCH
.cf = CHANGE FILE
.cl = CHANGE LIBRARY
.fo = FOCUS
.ef = EXIT FOCUS
.es = EXIT SERVICE
  m = MODIFY (NOT .MO)
.kw = KWIC
.vk = VARIABLE KWIC
```

```
.fu = FULL
.ci = CITE
.se = SEGMENTS
.dl = DISPLAY DIFFERENT LEVELS
.np = NEXT PAGE
.pp = PREVIOUS PAGE
.fp = FIRST PAGE
.nd = NEXT DOCUMENT
.pd = PREVIOUS DOCUMENT
.fd = FIRST DOCUMENT
sav = SAVE ECLIPSE SEARCH
rec = RECALL ECLIPSE SEARCH
.so = SIGN OFF
.sp = PRINT SCREEN
.pr = PRINT DOCUMENT
.pa = PRINT ALL
  r = DISPLAY CURRENT SEARCH REQUEST
  p = NUMBER OF SCREENS IN CURRENT DOCUMENT
      FORMAT
  c = RETURN TO CLIENT IDENTIFICATION SCREEN
  t = TIME ELAPSED IN CURRENT RESEARCH
      SESSION
.co = COST
  h = HELP
```

It may help to remember that the dot commands each have two letters and that those two letters are the first two letters of the command if it is a one-word command (.fo for focus) or the first letter of each word for a two-word command (.ns for new search). One- or three-letter abbreviations for commands don't have a period in front of them. I am sure there is a good reason for this system. In lieu of adopting a consistent system of abbreviation, LEXIS prints and distributes handy little cards that list the abbreviated commands. You may want to obtain some of these or copy the list just given here to post near your computer, tattoo on the back of your hand, and so on.

Retrieving Documents by Citation

LEXIS offers two services that retrieve documents by citation: LEX-STAT (for statutes and administrative code sections) and LEXSEE (for everything else). You can also find documents by searching the citation segment in a file. This approach is more costly and less efficient than using LEXSEE or LEXSTAT but is especially useful when you only have partial citation information to work with or you are looking for a document that is not available through LEXSEE or LEXSTAT.

LEXSEE and LEXSTAT

LEXSEE and LEXSTAT retrieve documents by citation for $4 each. You do not have to choose a library or file to use them, but they will work from any library and file. In other words, you may use LEXSEE or LEXSTAT from the library and file menu screens or while using any library and file. They can retrieve documents from the same or other libraries and files than the one you are using.

How To Retrieve Documents Using LEXSTAT or LEXSEE:
Simply type LEXSTAT (for statutes or administrative code sections) or LEXSEE (for other documents), followed by the document's citation, and press Enter. The first page of the document will be displayed and you can look through the full text using page commands and/or FOCUS (see Chapter 5).

To see a list of acceptable citation formats for documents available through LEXSTAT, enter LEXSTAT, and then enter H (for help). A list of citation formats for commonly requested documents follows this section. When entering citations in LEXIS for LEXSEE,

LEXSTAT, or other purposes, capitalization, spacing, and periods within the abbreviation in a cite don't matter (although you do need spaces before and after numbers, to "tell" LEXIS where the number begins and ends). 23 a2d 1 is as acceptable to LEXIS as 23 A.2d 1. To further streamline the process, you can trim LEXSTAT down to LXT if you like. For example, LEXSTAT 42 U.S.C.S. 1984 will produce the same result as LXT 42 uscs 1984.

The following documents are among those available through LEXSTAT, using the following citation formats:

PUBLICATION	FORMAT
Federal Statutes	21 us code 42 (the first number is the title and the second is the section)
California, Louisiana, New York, Maryland, and Texas statutes	These states' statutes require a topic abbreviation in their citation to be retrieved by LEXSTAT: see Appendix A for list. A Texas tax statute, for example, must have the code topic "tax" in addition to the section number; tx tax 1.01 is a valid citation for LEXSTAT purposes. Tx 1.01 is not.
Other state statutes	nc code 141.16 (the first two letters are the postal code for the state, and the number is the section number)
Code of Federal Regulations	49 cfr 110 (the first number is the title, second is the section)
Federal Register	55 fr 36612
State administrative code	21 xx admin 13 (replace xx with the state's postal code: ny admin, for example. Not all state administrative codes are available on-line.)
US Constitution	uscs const amend 1 (the uscs is because the constitution is in uscs on LEXIS)

■ Couldn't you just search for your citation in a library and file instead of bothering with this LEXSEE and LEXSTAT business? *Yes!*
The good folks at LEXIS who have their eyes on shiny new red
BMWs won't mind a bit if you do, since they will get to bill you
$19 to $91 more (depending on what file you use) per search than
if you had used the LEXSEE or LEXSTAT service. ■

 The following documents are available through LEXSEE,
using the following citation formats:

DOCUMENT	FORMAT
Cases	volume number followed by reporter abbreviation and page number: example, 101 us 1. See Appendix D for reporter abbreviations.
Documents in Federal Register	49 fr 20345 (first number is title, second is page)
Federal Tax materials Revenue Rulings Revenue Procedure Private Letter Rulings	rev rul 79-1 rev proc 81-1 plr 7652383
SEC no-action letters	1994 sec no-act lexis 123
Federal Energy Commission Decision	47 ferc p34, 091
Law review articles	56 neb l rev 1 (see Appendix D for LEXSEE abbreviations for law reviews)
ALR annotations	34 alr3d 1
Any document with a LEXIS cite	use the LEXIS cite: i.e., 1994 us lexis 12345

Getting Out of LEXSEE or LEXSTAT

When you are through viewing your retrieved documents, enter `.es` to exit the LEXSEE or LEXSTAT service and return to the screen you started on. Alternatively, enter `resume`, which will give you a menu of "places" (libraries, files, and services) you've been during the current research session and let you return to any of them. If there is only one choice, LEXIS will return to it rather than showing the option screen.

Searching with Terms and Connectors

LEXIS allows you to search the full text of any document in its database. This means that you can search for any word that appears anywhere in a document (actually, there are a few extremely common words, called *stop words,* that LEXIS will not let you search for because doing so would be useless and would tie up the system for impossibly long periods of time—see Appendix B for a full list). Full-text searching means that you can find things that were not included in print indexes. You can search for absolutely anything, not just the terms an indexer thought were important.

How to Search for a Single Term

To ask LEXIS to search for a term in a document, you just type it in on the query screen (see Figure 3.2), which appears after you have selected a library and file. Move the cursor to the end of the term and press Enter (see "Entering and Editing Commands," earlier in this chapter, for details on making corrections, etc.). Note that LEXIS screens often direct you to push the Transmit key: this is your Enter or Return key.

LEXIS will search all the documents in the file you selected and inform you of how many documents "satisfy your request," meaning that they contain the term you searched for (see Figure 3.3).

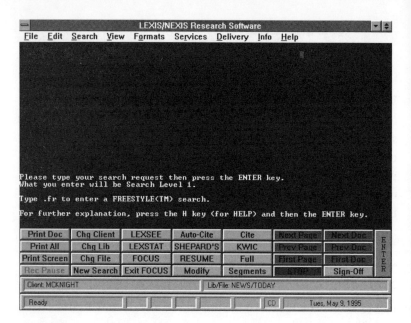

Figure 3.2

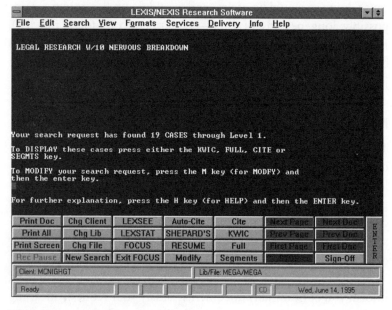

Figure 3.3

If you press Enter at this point, the first page of the first document will be displayed. When you press Enter again, the next few lines of the document that contain the term for which you searched will be displayed (see Figure 3.4).

Pressing Enter again takes you to the next portion of the text where your term appears, and so on, until the first pages of all the documents and all the parts of the documents where the term you searched for appears have been displayed. You can select a display mode that will allow you to see the full text of the retrieved documents or a list of their citations or to browse through them in other ways (see Chapter 5).

Plural and Possessive Terms: LEXIS finds singular, possessive, and regular plural forms (those formed by adding *s* or *es* to a word or by changing a *y* to *ies*) of terms automatically. Thus when you

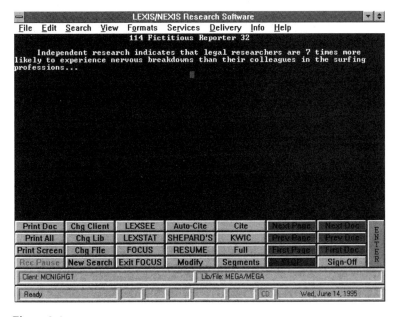

Figure 3.4

search for "cat," you are also searching for "cats," "cats'," and "cat's." When you search for "elephants," you get "elephant," and so on.

LEXIS does not find irregular plurals (such as "men" or "octopi"). If you want LEXIS to find such terms, you have to write them into your search.

TO FIND	SEARCH FOR
lumberjack or lumberjacks or lumberjack's or lumberjacks'	lumberjack
man or men or man's or men's	man or men
county or counties	county

Equivalents: LEXIS will automatically look for certain equivalent forms of terms. For the most part, these are numerical equivalents and abbreviations of dates, states, legal terms, or organizations. Appendix C contains a complete list of equivalents for which LEXIS searches automatically.

Combining Search Terms (Using Terms and Connectors)

If you've never used a full-text database, being able to search for a single term is impressive. But wait! There's more. You can search for more than one term at the same time, *and* specify the relationship between the positions of the terms. You can combine any terms you like (except the "stop" words listed in Appendix B) using the following connectors:

OR

AND

W/# (within # or fewer terms of each other)

PRE/#

W/SEG

NOT W/#

NOT W/SEG

AND NOT

These connectors specify the relationship between terms on either side of them. The relationship specified by each of the connectors is as follows.

OR: Using OR between two terms means that LEXIS will retrieve all documents in the file you are searching that contain either or both of the terms. Suppose, for example, that you search for "x OR y OR z." Suppose also that the following documents are among those in the file you are searching:

```
Document 1          Document 2          Document 3
blah blah blah      blah blah blah      blah blah blah
X blah blah.        y blah blah.        xyz.
```

Your search would retrieve all three of these documents because each of them has one or more of the terms you are searching for. You can string together as many terms as you like with OR between them, and LEXIS will retrieve any documents that contain any one or more of those terms.

AND: Using AND between terms means that *all* of the terms must appear at some point in the document. Suppose that you are searching the same file as in the OR example above and that you search for "x AND y AND z." This search will retrieve only the third document, since it is the only one with all the terms you asked for.

W/# (or NOT W/#): W/# is used to specify how close together the terms must be. The symbol # is the maximum number of terms that you want to be between the terms to be retrieved. You can use any number from 1 to 255 with the W/ connector. You cannot use W/ by itself (without a number).

If you search for "x W/5 y," LEXIS will retrieve documents in which the terms x and y appear within five words of each other. They may be in any order. They may be right beside each other or have one, two, three, or four words between them. Stop words (listed in Appendix B) don't count. As far as LEXIS is concerned, a "word" is anything with a space before and after it. Each of these is one word:

> tree
>
> 9
>
> $
>
> hush-puppy
>
> 6,007,899,999
>
> N.A.S.A.

To complicate things a little, certain punctuation marks are treated like spaces for purposes of counting "words." Parentheses and hyphens are treated as spaces. Thus, "up-to-date" counts as three words, as does "243(b)(4)."

PRE/#: PRE/# works just like W/# except that the terms must be in the order you give them (with the W/# connector they can be in any order). If you search for "x W/1 y," LEXIS looks for documents where x appears immediately before y *or* y appears immediately before x. If you search for "x PRE/1 y," LEXIS looks only for documents in which x appears immediately before y, *not* those in which y comes immediately before x.

W/SEG (or NOT W/SEG): Segments are parts of documents, like the opinion or citation of a case. There are different types of segments in different types of documents. Segments are described and explained in detail in Chapter 4. Suffice it to say at this point that the W/SEG connector lets you find terms that appear in the same segment. The NOT W/SEG connector lets you find terms that do not appear in the same segment. After you read Chapter 4 you will have a better idea of why you might care about this.

AND NOT: Sometimes you write a great search but you keep getting something you don't want in addition to what you do want. The AND NOT connector lets you eliminate specific things you do not want without giving up the part of the search that is retrieving what you do want. If you search for "x AND NOT y," you will get only those documents that have x *but not* y in them.

ATLEAST: The ATLEAST connector lets you limit your search to retrieve only documents that contain your search terms at least the number of times you specify. A search using the ATLEAST connector looks something like this:

> atleast 10 (adhesion w/5 contract)

The terms that you want to appear at least # times need to be in parentheses after the ATLEAST connector. You can add other parts to the search outside the parentheses and they will not be affected by the ATLEAST connector. For example, you could search for

> atleast 10 (adhesion w/5 contract) and truck

This would retrieve documents that contain the word "truck" at least one time and the word "adhesion" within five words of "contract" at least 10 times.

■ The ATLEAST connector is useful for finding especially relevant documents among a big pool of somewhat relevant documents. If your search retrieves an unworkable number of documents and you can't think of a good way to modify it without losing things you want, ATLEAST can pull out the documents that are likely to

(continued)

> **deal most closely with your issue, by virtue of mentioning it the most. This is especially important when your search involves very common terms. If you search for x and y and retrieve 900 documents, you can add the modification "and atleast 30 (x and y)." See Chapter 5 for an explanation of how to modify a search and why it is better to modify than do a new search. ■**

You can use ATLEAST to good effect as part of a modification or FOCUS request. Remember that every modification must begin with a connector.

Phrase Searching

To search for a phrase ("if we were all wiener dogs, our problems would be solved"), simply type it in. You don't need quotes or connectors between the terms if you want it to appear exactly as you typed it.

The Order of Processing

When you use more than one connector in a search, LEXIS has a specific order in which it processes your requests:

1. OR
2. W/#, PRE/#, NOT W/#
3. W/SEG
4. NOT W/SEG
5. AND
6. AND NOT

If there is more than one of any one category (say, three ORs), they are processed from left to right. If there is more than one of the # connectors (W/#, PRE/#, NOT W/#), the one with the smallest number is performed first. If the numbers are the same, they are done left to right. In other words, if you search for "x W/10 y W/2 z W/5 q W/5 r", y W/2 z will be processed first because it is the smallest number connector. z W/5 q will be processed next because it is the next smallest. It goes before q W/5 r because it is to the left of it. x W/10 y comes last because it contains the largest number.

What Difference Does the Order of Processing Make? The difference between finding what you want and not even coming close. If you search for "a AND b OR c," you will not get documents that do not have an a in them. You will get documents that have an a and either b or c or both. This may or may not have been what you intended, but it is what you'll get. Awareness of the impact of order of processing on your searches is crucial.

A search such as "a OR b W/10 c AND d BUT NOT f W/5 g" will involve several steps. First, LEXIS looks for documents with either a or b. If there are none, the search is over since OR is processed first and there will be nothing for the other connectors to operate on if the product of that first operation is zippo. Changing one connector (like so: "a OR b W/10 c OR d BUT NOT f w/5 g") can give entirely different results. Now if there are no documents containing a OR b, you may still find something (documents with d BUT NO f within five terms of g), while with the first search you could not. Most researchers cannot readily envision this without a pencil and paper and/or a small but shooting pain over one eye. Yet searches much more lengthy and complicated than this one are often the only way to find the specific information you need. The next section offers a solution that can help ease that shooting pain and improve the accuracy of your searches enormously.

Using Parentheses to Clarify the Order of Processing: You can make LEXIS process connectors the way *you* want it to by using parentheses. Parentheses indicate that terms within them should be processed together before being processed with other terms outside the parentheses. For example, "(a AND b) OR c" will give a significantly different result than the same search without the parentheses. It will retrieve documents containing both a and b, documents containing only c, or documents containing all three. Without the parentheses, no document without a would be retrieved.

You can use multiple parentheses, and even parentheses *within* parentheses, to further specify the order of processing in more complicated searches. The principle is the same. Terms grouped within the inner parentheses are combined first and then combined with other terms in the larger parentheses, and so on.

Universal Characters: Two universal characters are available to help you find close variations of a word. The exclamation point (!) affixed at the end of a term you enter gives you the root you enter with any ending at all, or none. For example, "run!" retrieves "run," "runner," "running," "runs," and probably some other words beginning with "run" that I can't think of. This is a handy solution to many problems, including how to retrieve all possible subsections of a statute ("243!" gets you 243.1, 243.1, 678(b), and so on). The exclamation point can only be used at the end of a term ("run!" will work, "r!n" will not).

For variations *within* a word, use an asterisk (*). The asterisk gives you *one* character variation; "r*n" gets you "run" or "ran," but not "rain." The asterisk can stand for any one character *or no character*. Thus "sa*d" retrieves "said" or "sad." You can use as many asterisks as you like within a word, but you cannot use one as the first character in a word ("*un" will not work). An asterisk can be used at the end of a word, but it operates differently than it would within the word, in that it will not retrieve words with no character in the asterisked space as it does if used within a word ("sa*d" retrieves "sad," but "sun*" does not retrieve "sun").

Natural Language Searching (Freestyle)

In addition to the terms and connectors (or Boolean) method, you can search LEXIS files using Freestyle, which lets you enter your terms in natural language without any connectors. For example, instead of searching for "class x felony W/25 and maximum sentence," you can search for "what is a class x felony and what is the maximum sentence for committing one?"

Using Freestyle

To switch over to the Freestyle mode from the Boolean mode, enter
.fr. Then enter your search query using any terms you choose. You
can enter the query in the form of a sentence ("what is the principal
export of Czechoslovakia") or just throw in some terms, heedless of
order or relationship ("Czechoslovakia principal export"). Either
way, Freestyle throws out the terms too common to be searched and
hunts for the rest. While LEXIS assumes that you are competent
enough to review your Boolean search before pressing Enter, it seems
to feel that you need prompting in Freestyle, so when you enter your
Freestyle query it will offer you, rather annoyingly, a chance to edit
your search. You have to press Enter again to actually run the search.

How Freestyle Works

Freestyle selects documents to retrieve based on the number of times
your search terms appear in them, multiplied by an "importance"
factor for each term that is based on how often the term appears in
the file you are searching. LEXIS assumes, reasonably enough, that
the more often a term appears in the file, the less likely it is to be of
use to you in flagging documents containing the specific issue for
which you are searching.

Specifying Mandatory Terms

To keep Freestyle from ignoring some of your search terms in favor
of others that appear more frequently, you must specify which search
terms you insist be included in retrieved documents. Since Freestyle
looks for the most instances of your search terms (multiplied by the
term's "importance," which is inversely related to how often the term
appears in the database you are searching—i.e., the more often it appears the less important it is), the entire group of documents it retrieves may contain as few as one of your search terms, with that
single term appearing enough times that Freestyle ranks these documents highest in hits. To be sure that all the documents retrieved

contain a particular term (rather than just a lot of instances of any of the terms you entered), you must specify that the term is "mandatory" by choosing option =2 after you enter your query the first time and before you press Enter again to confirm that it is correct. You will be prompted to type in the mandatory terms you choose and to press Enter again to run the search.

Freestyle Retrieves a Limited Number of Documents

You can select the limit. Freestyle automatically retrieves only 25 documents unless you change the default limit to any number between 1 and 1,000 by choosing option =5 from the Freestyle search options screen, which appears after you enter your search and before you press Enter again to start the search.

Phrases in Freestyle

Enclose phrases (words that must be together) in your Freestyle query within quotation marks, otherwise they will not stay together but will be searched for as individual terms. No quotation marks are necessary for phrases when using terms and connectors.

Restricting Your Freestyle Search

To restrict your search, type in your query and press Enter. Then choose "<=3> Enter/edit restrictions (e.g. date)" from the menu. Follow the on-screen instructions to enter your restrictions. All the tips on restricting your search to these segments in terms and connectors mode (discussed earlier in this chapter) apply equally here, but note that only five restrictions (date, court, name, judges, and counsel) are available in Freestyle. There are many more restrictions available in terms and connectors mode.

Viewing Your Freestyle Results

Freestyle-retrieved documents are displayed in the order of how many "hits" they contain (most to least). You can change this so that documents are displayed in the more familiar reverse chronological

order (as they are in terms and connectors mode) by entering
.sort or by choosing Option 4 on the screen that announces your
results after you enter a search.

In addition to the usual display formats for viewing your results (CITE, KWIC, FULL, and VAR-KWIC), you can use the Su-
perKWIC mode, which shows the portions of text that contain the
most instances of your search terms close together. To use Super-
KWIC, type .sk.

Otherwise Freestyle results can be viewed, modified, and
printed in the same way as Boolean search results.

.where and .why

Type .where to see which of your retrieved documents contain
which of your search terms. As explained above, the retrieved documents do not necessarily contain all of your search terms. Figure 3.5
shows a .where display.

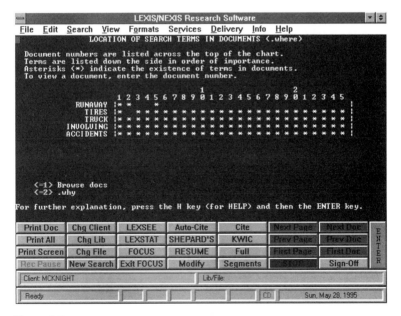

Figure 3.5

Type .why to see how many documents Freestyle actually found ("documents matched"), as opposed to how many it displayed, which is limited by the default display limit. The .why feature also shows you how many of the documents displayed and how many of the documents "matched" contained each of your search terms. Figure 3.6 shows a .why display.

Freestyle versus Boolean

Freestyle saves you the trouble of worrying about choosing the appropriate terms and connectors and about the order of processing that bedevils Boolean searches, but you have a lot less control over what you find. Freestyle is good for broad exploratory searches and for a last-ditch effort when you aren't having luck with your Boolean search or want to supplement it, but I can't recommend it as a complete replacement for Boolean searching when you need to find

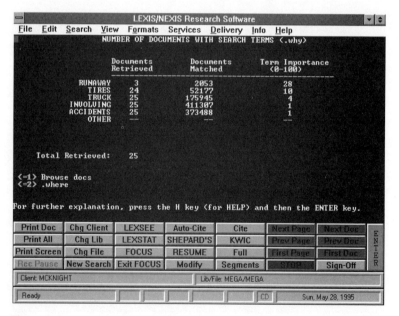

Figure 3.6

everything that's "out there" on a given topic. Freestyle is easy and fun for initial and final supplemental overviews, allowing you to cast a search net vaguely and broadly and almost always catch *something*, but Boolean is the clear winner when it comes to retrieving specific, comprehensive results. Boolean allows you to specify segments to be searched and precise relationships between your search terms for a higher degree of accuracy than is possible with Freestyle.

CHAPTER 3.   QUICK REFERENCE PAGE

.ns = New Search
.cf = Change File
.cl = Change Library
 H = Help

LEXSTAT retrieves statutes and administrative code sections—example: LEXSTAT 22 U.S.C. 22567.

LEXSEE retrieves everything else—example: LEXSEE 419 U.S. 345.

.es or Resume to exit LEXSEE or LEXSTAT

CONNECTORS	ORDER OF PROCESSING OF CONNECTORS
OR	1. OR
AND	2. W/#, PRE/#, NOT W/# (smallest # is
W/#	processed first)
NOT W/#	3. W/SEG
PRE/#	4. NOT W/SEG
W/SEG	5. AND
NOT W/SEG	6. AND NOT
AND NOT	When there is more than one of the same
ATLEAST	category, LEXIS processes left to right.

Universal Characters
  ! used only at end of word, gives any endings (run!)
  * used anywhere in word except as first character. Lets one
    character vary (may be blank except if at end of word).

4

Fine-Tuning Your Research

THIS CHAPTER COVERS THREE WAYS TO FINE-TUNE
YOUR SEARCHES ONCE YOU ALREADY HAVE THE
BASICS (SEE CHAPTER 3):

Date restrictions

Segments

Modifying a search

The .more feature

Date Restrictions

You can easily write a search that will limit documents retrieved to
those from a particular date or range of dates. You must have a
search (at least one term) to begin with; you can't search for a date
alone. To restrict your search to documents with a certain date (say
April 5, 1990), just add `and date is April 5, 1990` to the
search. For example, you could search the major newspapers file in
NEXIS for `corporate takeover and date is April
5, 1990`. You can restrict searches to retrieve documents before a
certain date (date bef ——), after a certain date (date aft ——), on a
certain date (date is ——), in a range of dates (date aft —— and
date bef ——), or even outside a range of dates (date bef —— and
date aft ——). You can substitute the < symbol for `bef`, the > symbol for `aft`, and the = symbol for `is` if you prefer).

LEXIS accepts a wide range of date notations:

TIME PERIOD	FORM ACCEPTED BY LEXIS	EXAMPLES
years	A given year can be a four-digit or two-digit number (1989 or 89). You do not have to specify a month or day.	1989 89
months	You have to specify a year. Months can be spelled out, given as numbers (with or without a zero before a single-digit number), or abbreviated with three or four letters: Jan, Feb (or Febr), Mar, Apr, May, Jun, Jul, Aug, Sep (or Sept), Oct, Nov, Dec.	April, 1990 Apr, 90 04/90 4/90 4-1990
days	Use a numerical date, including a month and a year in one of the forms above.	April 5, 1990 4/5/90

Segments

A segment is a specific part of a document: a case's citation or the opinion or dissent, for example. Each type of document has different segments. Only cases have Judge segments, for example.

The *LEXIS Product Guide* has sample documents and segment descriptions for various types of documents (and because of the size of the *Guide*, looking them up is good exercise, too). To display a list of segments available in any particular file, type . se and press Enter while you are in the file in question.

Note that a segment in any given document may be empty—for example, a case may have no dissent in the Dissent segment because no one dissented. This doesn't mean that the segment isn't available in that type of document or file, just that the segment is empty in that particular document.

What Are Segments Good For?

You can limit your search to particular segments for more precise results in some cases. For example, let's say you want to retrieve Roe v.
Wade and you don't have a citation for it. If you just search for Roe v.
Wade, you get hundreds of cases that mention Roe v. Wade but aren't
it. Picking out the one that *is* Roe v. Wade could be very time con-
suming. You can avoid this problem by searching for Roe v. Wade in
the Name segment. This search retrieves only those cases where Roe
v. Wade is the citation of the case, not all those where it is mentioned
in the opinion. Note, by the way, that it actually works much better to
search by party names with a connector (usually "AND") between
them than with a "v." This is because the parties' full names are usually used in the name of the case, but not in the name by which the
case is commonly known. "Roe v. Wade" in the Name segment of the
Supreme Court cases file doesn't actually retrieve Roe v. Wade because of this; "Roe AND Wade" does.

How to Do a Segment Search

To do a segment search, type the name or abbreviation of the segment, followed (include a space or not—it doesn't matter) by the
terms you are looking for in that segment. For example, to find cases
where Justice Learned Hand wrote a dissenting opinion, search for
`dissentby(hand)`.

Segment Tricks

TECHNIQUE	EXAMPLE
You can use segments to find a case when you know the names of a party but don't have a full citation.	`name(mcgillicudy w/5 bertha)`
Find all the opinions written by a particular judge.	`writtenby(scalia)`—first names are not included in the Judge

(continued)

segment, so you may have to limit your search to a specific court and/or date range if the name is common.

Find cases in which a certain attorney or firm appeared (make a good impression in an interview, size up the competition, check out what old friends are up to).

`counsel(biggs and bucks)` or `counsel(john /5 doe)`

Tips for Searching Specific Segments

Some segments have special characteristics you need to know about in order to make fullest use of them.

Name Segment: When searching for personal names, use `PRE/5` between the first and last names to account for middle names. Although even his mother never calls him by his full name, the court may, and John Alodocius Theopolis Francis "Bud" Doe won't turn up under "John Doe."

When searching for case names, use "AND" instead of "v." To find the Godzilla v. Megalon case, search for `name(godzilla and megalon)`. This way you can retrieve the case commonly referred to as Godzilla v. Megalon, which is really named John P. Godzilla and the Cheesy Movie Monsters Local v. Megalon Enterprises.

Shorten really long names to their most unusual parts. If you want a case where one of the parties' names is seven lines long, just pick out the most unusual words and search for those. If you want to find the Smith and Brown Construction Company's Midwest Tristate Geodesic Triphasic Widget Division v. Doe case, try `name(Geodesic Triphasic)`. It's quicker and much less prone to typographical disaster. Very common terms just slow the system down and aren't much help in retrieving the specific document you want.

Writtenby, Opinionby, Concurby, and Dissentby Segments: Only last names of judges are given, so if your judge has a common last name, you may need to limit your search by court and/or date range to get only the one you want. Note that the Writtenby segment contains Concurby, Dissentby, and Opinionby—think of it as the "anything written by" segment.

Counsel Segment: The same cautions as those noted in the Name segment apply to searching for attorney names in this segment. When searching for firm names, try using names strung together with "AND" if the official firm name doesn't work: for Smith, Helms, Mullis and Moore, use `smith and helms and mullis and moore`—this way a new partner doesn't throw you off.

Courts Segment: Your choice of files will often narrow the courts covered sufficiently, but if you need to specify a court in a file that has more than one, just search for the court's name in the Court segment—for example, `courts(eastern and north carolina)`. It is quicker if you skip very common words in the name (such as "court" and "district"). You must write out the name of the state in a segment search rather than using an abbreviation or postal code.

Segments that Contain Numbers: Some segments commonly contain numerical information. For example, the net sales and eps-growth (percentage increase in earnings per share over last 5 years) segments. You can use greater than, less than, and equals symbols to find particular numbers or ranges. For example, you can search for companies with `net sales < 100,000`.

Docket Numbers: Docket numbers usually consist of two numbers. The first is a two-digit year number. The other number is the number of the case on the year's docket. These numbers are sometimes separated with a hyphen (89-241) and sometimes with letters (89 cu 241); if you have trouble retrieving a case by docket, try using AND between the numbers instead of letters or a hyphen. This eliminates many misunderstandings that poor, simple LEXIS may have.

Modifying a Search

$ Once you see the documents your ever-so-skillfully-crafted search retrieves, you may want to change your search requirements a little. You may have retrieved too many documents to read, or fewer than you expected and would like, or many that are clearly irrelevant. Instead of doing a new search, which will cost you $24 to $95 minimum, you can modify your search for no additional search charge (only connect time).

$ Before you modify, take a quick look at what your original search retrieved to see if a clear pattern or mistake is apparent. See Chapter 5 for tips on quick and efficient review of your search results.

■ Note that although it is less expensive to review results off-line than on-line, it can end up costing you more if you don't look over those results enough to know whether you want to modify before you sign off and lose your chance. Once you leave your search results by signing off or doing another search, it's too late to modify them. You'll have to do (and pay for) a new search. For maximum savings, review your results quickly (see tips in Chapter 5) and consider possible modifications *before* you sign on. There will always be some surprises that will require you to think on your feet, but it is better to plan calmly and carefully before the meter starts running when you sign on. ■

By starting with a broad search and modifying after you check your results, you are less likely to miss relevant documents than you might if you started out with a narrower search. At least you will be aware of the larger pool of possible documents. You can modify up to 255 times! Doing several different modifications can help you keep a close eye on what you are eliminating and including with each change. If you put all your possible modifications in one search, it is hard to tell which part brought your pool of documents from ten zillion to zero. The breakdown will be clearer if you modify a little bit, one step at a time. For example, if your original search retrieves an absurd number of documents on x, you might modify it to include a date restriction, and then again to retrieve only those documents that mention x within ten words of y.

How to Modify a Search

Once you have entered a search and retrieved some sort of result, type m and press Enter to modify. Note that MODIFY is not a dot command—you just type m, not .m. When you enter m to modify, the system tells you what your search is so far and tells you to add your modification. (See Figure 4.1.)

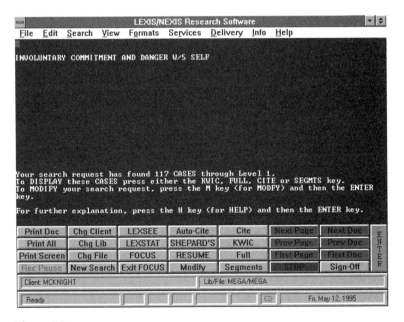

Figure 4.1

Note that you type in only the modification to be added to the old search and that you must start your modification with a connector (see the section on terms and connectors in Chapter 3). LEXIS will not accept a modification that does not begin with a connector.

Levels

Once you have entered a modification, the results are displayed as Level 2 results. Another modification to the same search will result in Level 3 results, and so on. You can go back and view an earlier level at any point. This is yet another benefit of modifying rather than doing a new search: all previous results are deleted and replaced by the new results when you do a new search. To display a different level, enter .dl and the number of the level you wish to see. For example, enter .dl2 to see the second level. You can also print any level by moving to that level before issuing your print request (see Chapter 7 on printing and downloading).

Warning: Modification and the Order-of-Processing Trap

Because of the order in which connectors are processed (see Chapter 3), you can't always modify a search to do exactly what you could with a new search. For example, suppose you search for "x AND y." After browsing the results, you wish you had left out x and used a instead. If you modify the search with "OR a," you will only get documents that have x *and* either y or a, since ORs are processed first; an OR modification only modifies the *last* term in the search. You can't get rid of x without doing a new search.

There are ways to get around this problem. You can't eliminate it completely, but it helps to put the term you are most likely to want to try alternatives for last, so that an OR connector will be able to act on it. You can also use parentheses in your original search to keep things in the groupings you prefer. For example, instead of an original search for "x AND y," search for "(x AND y)." This way when it turns out that x doesn't exist in the database, you can modify with

"OR a" and get some documents if there are some containing a. Without the parentheses in the original search, the "OR a" modification will retrieve no documents, since we've established there are no documents containing x and LEXIS will be searching for x *AND* (y OR a), meaning that each document retrieved must contain x.

This sort of problem is one reason that computerized legal research results can be deceptive. You enter x AND y and modify with OR a, and if you haven't read all about connectors and also had a lot of coffee, you are likely to assume that "no documents satisfy your search query" means that there are no documents containing x and y, or any containing a. In fact there may be a zillion documents containing a, but you have no idea they exist because they don't have an x or y in them (picture LEXIS saying, angry-teenager style, "*but you said . . .*"). This kind of disaster is less likely to occur in book research (although it can certainly be done), where you have indexes and tables of contents to give you a hint if there is something *close.* The wonder of high-tech computerized legal research is that you can find nearly anything—and you can miss nearly anything too.

■ If you are ever kidnapped by aliens and held for years in solitary confinement or have a really long wait in the checkout lane at the Piggly-Wiggly, you can try to work out all the permutations of the order of processing of connectors. Otherwise you may never get around to it. You will not be alone, and you can bumble along pretty well anyway as long as you make careful use of parentheses in your searches. Don't tempt fate by not bothering to learn either the order of processing or how to use parentheses. See Chapter 3 for everything you need to know about the order of processing and parentheses. You can probably learn it easily while you're microwaving your next frozen burrito. ■

Modifying a Modification

You can modify up to 255 times in a row. It can be fairly challenging to keep track of the ramifications of the order of processing of connectors mentioned earlier, but if you manage that, multiple modifications allow you to get a good feel for what documents are out there without paying for multiple searches. When you do a search and then modify it and then modify it again, that second modification operates on the modified search, not the original search.

Replacing a Modification

If you want to *replace* a modification you have already entered, as opposed to modifying it, you can do so by entering the number of the modification you want to modify followed by m and then entering the replacement modification. Are you getting that headache again? No? Well, how about this, then: when you replace a modification you destroy all the modifications that followed it up to the current one (like a time travel movie where the hero has to keep the past the same or the present will scoot right out from under him). Say, for example, that under the influence of extreme pressure or pharmaceutical stimulus you have modified a search 253 times, and you suddenly decide that you wish you had done a different modification the 14th time. So you enter 14m and replace (change) your 14th modification to read "or kumquats." Your Level-15 results will change accordingly (the 14th modification produces the Level-15 results—the original search is Level 1, the first modification is Level 2, . . .). Levels 16 through 254 disappear—*zip!*—down a wormhole in space, never to be seen again. This may be of no concern to you at all, of course, particularly considering the state of mind that brought you to this pass in the first place, but it is something to be aware of.

> ■ When should you use FOCUS instead of MODIFY, or the other way around? MODIFY is useful when you want to change the pool of documents retrieved. FOCUS lets you search for things within a pool you are happy with (at least for the time being). FOCUS can't give you any new documents to work with; MOD-

IFY can. FOCUS lets you highlight and go quickly to terms other than those you searched for; MODIFY does not. Multiple MODIFY requests for the same original search build on each other, while FOCUS requests do not, and thus FOCUS requests avoid the confusions of "stacked" searches interacting with each other. ■

What if you can't remember what you've already searched for and modified? Just enter the letter r (for request) to get a complete account of everything you did from the time you signed on until the moment that everything went blank. LEXIS will not even chide you for failing to pay attention. Press Enter to go back to the documents most recently retrieved, m and Enter to do another modification, .ns to do a new search, and so on. Your request will retrieve a screen something like Figure 4.2.

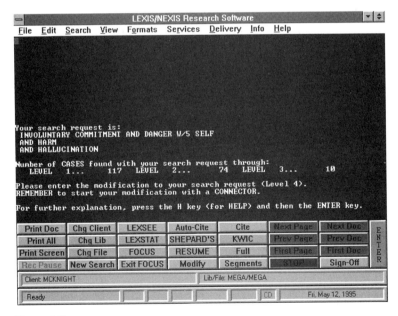

Figure 4.2

The .more Feature

The .more feature allows you to retrieve additional documents on the same subject as a given document by automatically creating a Freestyle search (see Chapter 3) based on the terms in that document. To use .more, simply type `.more` at the top of the screen of a document you are viewing and press Enter. LEXIS will formulate a Freestyle search and display it for you to edit. You can add or delete terms and specify mandatory terms so that the search includes the topics of interest to you (LEXIS is only "guessing" which terms are important) and press Enter to run the search. Type `.em` and press Enter to return to your original document.

The .more feature puts you into Freestyle mode. The number of documents .more retrieves depends on the Freestyle setting you have chosen, and you can manipulate the search that is formulated for you just like one you type yourself. (See Chapter 2 for more information on Freestyle searching.) After using .more you will remain in the Freestyle mode until you type `.bool` and press Enter to return to Boolean (terms and connectors) searching.

CHAPTER 4.   QUICK REFERENCE PAGE

Examples of date restrictions:

```
date bef 1989
date aft 6/91
date is 4/24/90
date aft 7/94 and date bef 10/94
```

.se for a list of segments available in file

Sample segment searches:

```
name(roe and wade)
name(john w/5 doe)
writtenby(scalia)
counsel(biggs and bucks)
court(supreme and united states)
```

```
.m   = Modify
.dl# = Display different level (example: .dl2)
.m#  = Replace modification # (example: .m2)
r    = Request list of what you've done since you signed on
```

5

Looking at What You've Found

THIS CHAPTER DEALS WITH HOW TO LOOK AT WHAT
YOU'VE RETRIEVED USING ANY KIND OF SEARCH
(SEE CHAPTERS 3 AND 4). IT COVERS:

On-line or off-line?

Display modes

Changing display modes

Display order

Browsing within a document

Moving between documents

Browsing administrative and statutory codes

Displaying different search levels

Pagination

Link

FOCUS

O NCE YOU have successfully executed a search request, the
system will report how many documents you have
found (see Figure 5.1).

If you have succeeded in retrieving a reasonable number of
documents (i.e., at least one and not more than you can look at before you retire) or if you haven't and need some idea of where you
might have gone wrong so you can modify your search appropri-

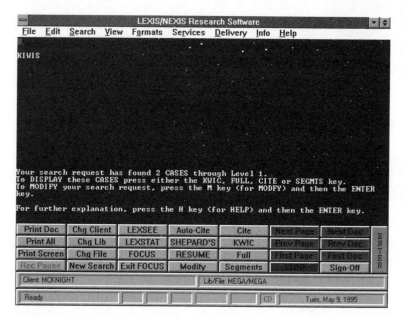

Figure 5.1

ately (see Chapter 4 for how to modify a search), your next step is to look at what you've found.

On-Line or Off-Line?

Having retrieved some documents, you can look at them on-line or off-line (by printing or downloading), or you can do a little of both. You have several choices:

 ◆ Print or download all the retrieved documents, and look at them after you sign off (Chapter 7 considers the mechanics and relative merits of printing and downloading). Printing and downloading are not free ($2 per document at the time of this writing, plus your paper, ink, and printer-maintenance costs to print).

◆ Print or download only the citations of the retrieved documents, and look them up in paper sources (this gives you the minimum possible print charges but means you must have access to print sources and take time to find and read through them).

◆ Read the documents in their entirety on-line.

◆ Review the retrieved documents quickly to evaluate their relevance. Modify your search as needed (see Chapter 4), and print or download cites or full text selectively.

The fourth option (quick evaluation and selective printing and/or downloading) is usually the most efficient strategy. You avoid unnecessary printing and downloading charges and also save considerable time by taking advantage of the browsing capabilities of LEXIS. Say, for example, that you need to review a case you retrieved to see what it says about a given statute. You can print or download the case and skim each page (maybe 30, 40, or more pages) to find where that statute is mentioned, or you can hit a few keys and go right to it on screen. Multiply this time saving by the number of documents you have to review and you can see that time savings can be enormous. You can still print a cite list and read the full text of relevant documents in print if you like.

$ Reviewing on-line lets you confirm the success of your search promptly, saving the expense and irritation of signing on again to redo your search. Since you pay a large fee each time you do a new search that you do not pay when you modify a search still on your screen, reviewing your search results while still on-line makes a lot of sense.

Display Modes

In order to look at the documents you have found on-line, you need to choose a display mode and use the browsing commands to move both between documents and within a document.

KWIC (Key Words in Context)

KWIC displays an excerpt of 50 words (not counting noise or stop words) surrounding your search terms, which are highlighted (see Figure 5.2, where the search term is "kiwis").

KWIC is the default display mode; it will be chosen for you if you press Enter to display the documents. To change to KWIC after you have selected another display mode, type . kw. KWIC is an especially efficient display mode for looking over what you've found. KWIC allows you to judge the relevance of retrieved documents and evaluate the efficacy of your search much more quickly than reading through each page of the documents retrieved.

VAR-KWIC

VAR-KWIC is just like KWIC, but with the number of words *you* select (from 1 through 999) around your search terms. Choose VAR-

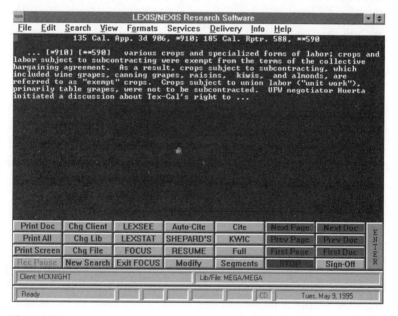

Figure 5.2

KWIC by typing `.vk##`, with ## being the number of words you select (for example, `.vk35`). If you type `.vk` without specifying a number, the system defaults to 50 words around your search terms.

FULL

FULL displays the full text of documents (see Figure 5.3).

To choose the FULL display mode, type `.fu`. FULL may give you more information than you need on a "first pass" through the materials you have retrieved and thus cost you extra time and money. Start with one of the other display modes to determine the relevance of the documents retrieved and decide whether your search needs to be modified or replaced. Once you are fairly certain you have the documents you want, you can use FULL to read them in their entirety. You may still want to print a hard copy of the document to work from. With a printed record you won't have to repeat

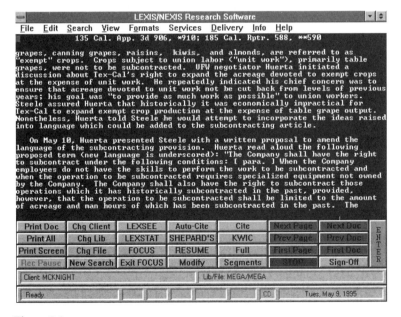

Figure 5.3

your search later to refresh your memory, an avoidable loss of still more time and money (see Chapter 12 for more information on printing, storing, and downloading).

CITE

CITE lists only citations of documents retrieved (see Figure 5.4).

Choose CITE by entering `.ci`. In many research situations CITE is an efficient display mode in which to begin reviewing your results, as it may allow you to eliminate some documents right away or alert you to a problem with your search (oh, say, nineteenth-century cases retrieved by your search for manufacturers' liability for rollerblading injuries).

While viewing citations, you can choose to see any document in KWIC format by entering the number at the beginning of the cite.

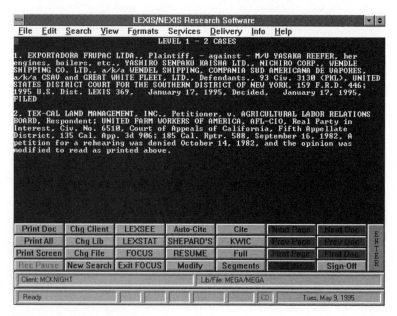

Figure 5.4

For example, to see a KWIC display of the second case on the citation display list in Figure 5.4, you would type 2 and press Enter.

SEGMENTS

SEGMENTS displays only requested segments of documents (see Chapter 4 for a full explanation of segments).

Choose the SEGMENTS display mode by typing .se. The system then shows you the segments available in the documents you have retrieved and prompts you to select one or more (see Figure 5.5).

To choose a segment, type its name as listed on the screen. For example, to display the disposition segment, type disposition and press Enter. This will result in the segment(s) you requested appearing directly below the identifying information for the case (as opposed to appearing in their normal positions in the case) (see Figure 5.6).

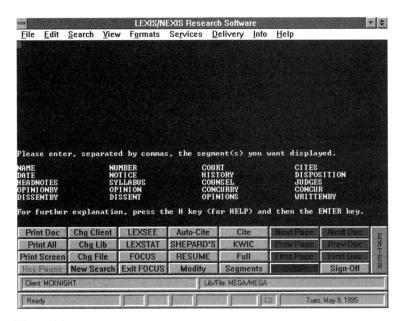

Figure 5.5

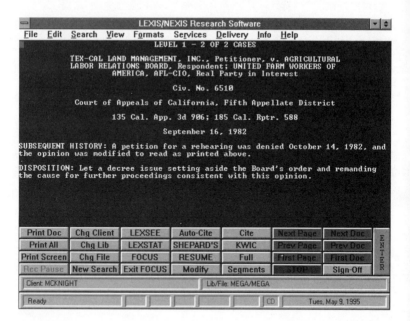

Figure 5.6

To choose more than one segment, separate them with commas; for example, you might select Date, Court, and Counsel. The system will then display the segments you requested, along with basic identifying information for each document retrieved. Some segments are not available in some documents and so will not appear on this list. For example, the Court segment, which identifies the court that handed down an opinion, is not available in a statute database, since statutes are created by the legislature and not by a court. Also, a given document may not have text in all segments.

SEGMENTS is an efficient choice where the information you are looking for can be limited to a particular segment of all documents, as when you wish to see opinions by certain judges or on certain dates, or when you are interested only in a given part of the documents you have found, such as the syllabi.

Changing Display Modes

You may enter a command for a new display mode at any time. For example, as noted earlier, if you are browsing a case in KWIC, the screen might look like Figure 5.7.

As before, to see the full text of the case you are viewing, simply type the command for full-text display mode, `. fu`, and press Enter. The full text of the case you were viewing will appear, beginning with the part of the document you were viewing when you gave the command (see Figure 5.8).

Default Display Mode: If you do not choose a display mode but simply press Enter, the system will choose the KWIC display mode for you. This is not a bad idea, since KWIC gives you a quick overview of what you've found (not as quick as CITE, but with more

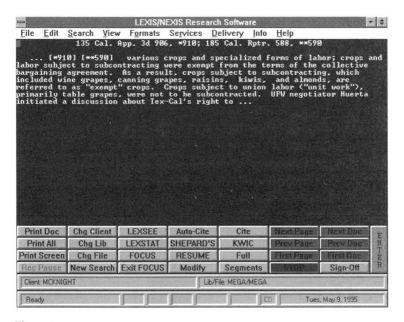

Figure 5.7

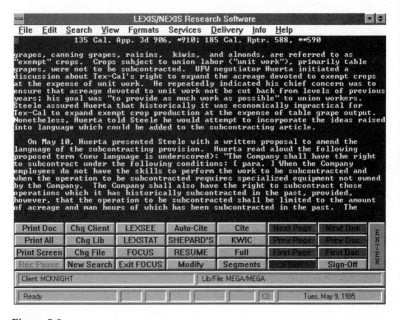

Figure 5.8

information). If you aren't sure what mode to use, you can't go far wrong with the KWIC default.

Display Order

Recent documents are ordinarily displayed before older documents (in reverse chronological order, as the pocket-protector-and-slide-rule set puts it). When cases from different courts or jurisdictions are retrieved, all the cases from the highest court are displayed first (newest to oldest), followed by the cases from the next court or jurisdiction (newest to oldest), and so on. Federal cases precede state cases, and state cases are listed alphabetically. Cases are not separated into districts or circuits. So, for example, the following cases would be ordered as shown:

U.S. Supreme Court 1994 case

U.S. Supreme Court 1980 case

U.S. Court of Appeals 1990 case

U.S. Court of Appeals 1989 case

Alaska Supreme Court 1993 case

California Supreme Court 1994 case

Statutes and administrative regulations are displayed in code-number order rather than by date, with federal law preceding state laws, and states listed in alphabetical order.

Browsing within a Document

Once you have chosen a display mode you will be rewarded with a list of citations or a part of a document. The following commands allow you to move within a document:

COMMAND	EFFECT	EXAMPLE
Enter	move to next page	
.np	move to next page	
#.np	move forward # pages	on page 7, type 3 .np and press Enter to go to page 10
.pp	move to previous page	
#.pp	move back # pages	on page 15, type 4 .pp and press Enter to go to page 11
.fp	move to first page	
Page Up	move back one page	
Page Down	move forward one page	

Moving between Documents

COMMAND	EFFECT	EXAMPLE
.nd	move to next document	
.pd	move to previous document	
.fd	first document	
#.nd	move forward # documents	from the 3rd document, type 2.nd to go to the 5th document
#.pd	move back # documents	from document 9, type 3.pd to go to document 6
#	go to document #	type 8 to go to document 8

You can also use page commands or the Enter key to move automatically from the last page of one document to the first page of the next, or vice versa. Of course, this method is inefficient unless you are already on the first or last page of one document when you wish to move to an adjacent one.

Browsing Administrative and Statutory Codes

If you retrieve a section of an administrative or statutory code, you can view other parts of the same code (even if you did not retrieve those parts in your search) by typing B. Note that it is not otherwise possible to view sections that you did not retrieve, and that BROWSE works only for codes. It does not, for example, allow you to move from one article to others in the same journal that were not retrieved by your original search.

Displaying Different Search Levels

If you have modified your search, you have created more than one level of retrieved documents (see Chapter 4). To view another of the levels, type .dl #, with # being the number of the level you wish to see. The system will display the first screen of the first case retrieved at that level.

Pagination

LEXIS page numbers and printed source page numbers ordinarily do not line up. A feature called *Star Paging* makes it possible to cite correct page numbers for cases in various reporters. Asterisks and numbers in brackets show where hard-copy reporter page breaks fall in a LEXIS case. For example, in the screen shown in Figure 5.9, the part of the opinion that begins with "The plaintiff had a bad fall . . ." begins on page 499 in Vermont Reports (Vt.) and on page 860 in the Atlantic Reports, 2d Series (A.2d). This is shown by the asterisks and numbers in brackets: the number with one asterisk always corresponds to the first reporter listed at the top of the screen, the number with two asterisks corresponds to the second reporter at the top of the screen, and so on (see Figure 5.9).

How to Move to a Particular Page

To retrieve a page from a particular reporter, check the top of a screen of the case to find how many asterisks denote the correct reporter and type p followed by that number of asterisks and the page number you wish to see. For example, to locate a quote that you know is on page 864 of the A.2d version of the case shown in Figure 5.9, type p**864 and press Enter (note that this command will work only when entered from a screen of that case). The system will automatically put the first part of the page for which you searched at the top of the screen.

If there are no alternative reporter versions for the case (only a LEXIS cite is given), type p*# to go to a particular LEXIS page (see Figure 5.10).

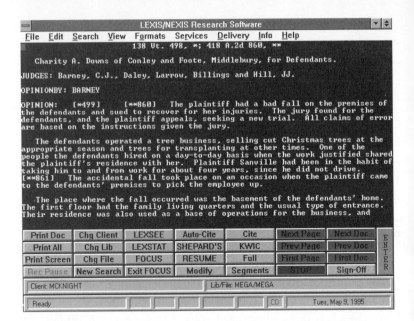

Figure 5.9

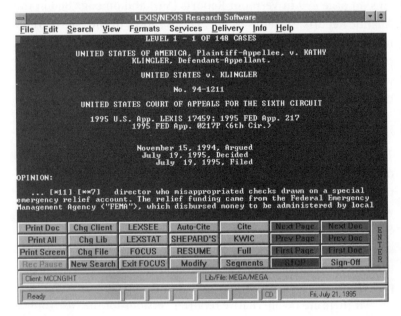

Figure 5.10

Star Paging may be available for a reporter even though it is not listed on the screen of a case you are viewing. Type `star` followed by the abbreviation of the reporter for which you would like to see pagination (for example, `star NE2d`) and press Enter. If available, this reporter's pagination will appear in your case and other paginations will be dropped. Note that Star Paging is not available in all documents; only for cases printed in major reporters.

How Many Pages Are in Your Document?

To see how many pages are in a document you are viewing, type `p` and press Enter. The service will tell you how many pages there are in the display mode you are using, so be sure to use FULL if you want the number of full pages, KWIC if you want the number of pages containing your search terms, and so on. If you entered the `p` command from a case you were viewing in KWIC, the result would look something like Figure 5.11.

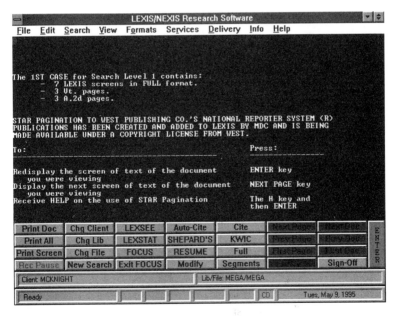

Figure 5.11

Link

When browsing cases on LEXIS, you will often come across an equal sign and a number in brackets (<=1>) beside a citation to another case. This is a link marker, which enables you to skip directly to the text of that case without "losing your place" in the current one.

You can view the full text of a case cited beside a link marker by clicking on its marker or typing = and the appropriate link-marker number. For example, to see Rich v. Tite-Knot Pine Mill from the screen shown in Figure 5.12, simply click on the link marker (the <=4>) *or* type =4 and press Enter. The first page of Rich will then be displayed in full text. To see Porreca v. Atlantic Refining Co., click on <=2> or type =2.

Once you have used link to jump to a case, you can read or download the case, or you can use FOCUS to look for particular

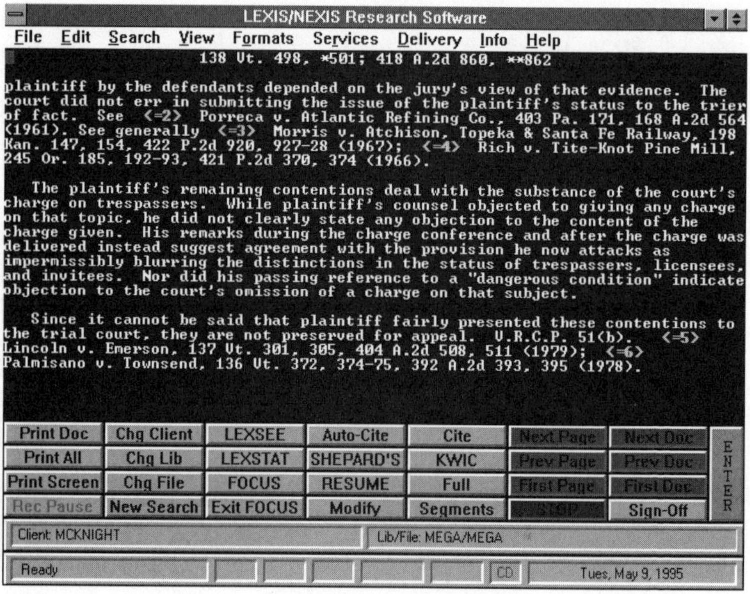

Figure 5.12

terms in it. When you are finished reviewing the linked case, you can return to the screen you were viewing when you issued the link command by typing .es (exit service) or resume and pressing Enter.

You can remove all link markers from sight by typing .linkoff and restore them by typing .linkon and pressing Enter.

FOCUS

FOCUS lets you locate specific terms within the documents you have found. From the screen telling you how many documents you have retrieved, you can type .fo followed by a search query (see Chapter 3 for a detailed explanation of formulating search queries). The system will show your original search and ask you to type in your FOCUS request, as in Figure 5.13.

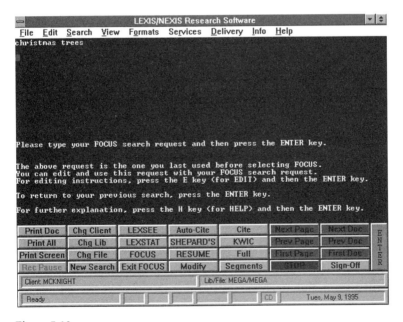

Figure 5.13

You may use any terms in your FOCUS search, whether they were included in your original query or not. If you want to hide the highlighting of your original search terms, delete them from the screen or type over them with your FOCUS search. They will not be highlighted in your results. If you do want to include them, simply move your cursor to the end of your original search request, which is already on the screen for you, and add your FOCUS terms with a connector.

■ Why would you *want* to hide the highlighting from your original search? Are you some kind of clutter fanatic? Could be. Lawyers as a group probably won't win a lot of mental hygiene prizes. But eliminating highlighting of common terms can save you a lot of time in locating what you really want to see, since the system insists on displaying each screen with a highlighted term. ■

The whole array of terms and connectors is at your disposal. You need not use your original search terms at all or limit your search to single terms.

■ Shortcut: If you aren't using your original search terms, save a little bit of time (maybe, say, the cost of a small bag of Cheez Doodles over the course of a month), by typing focus and a space and your FOCUS term (for example, focus widgets). This saves waiting for the system to display your original search and prompt you to enter your FOCUS search. Of course, this is no time saver if you are going to retype a lengthy search query. ■

Use as many terms and connectors as you like. FOCUS searches are constructed by the same rules as ordinary searches (see Chapter 3). Once you have typed in your FOCUS request and checked it for errors, press Enter. The system will respond with the number of items retrieved and you can display them in the standard display modes. Terms you searched for will be highlighted.

To do another FOCUS search once you are in FOCUS, just type a new query and press Enter. Once you have requested a FOCUS, the system regards whatever you type in as a new FOCUS request until you exit FOCUS by typing `.ef` and pressing Enter.

Exiting FOCUS

After using FOCUS, you must type `.ef` and press Enter to exit FOCUS and resume other functions. If you don't exit FOCUS, everything you type in is read by LEXIS as a FOCUS request.

What Is FOCUS Good For?

FOCUS saves you time and money by helping you locate relevant portions of documents quickly without an additional search charge.

$ You can essentially create your own file with your original search request and search it as many ways as you like for no extra search charges with FOCUS. Doing a new search instead of using FOCUS will add double digits to your bill for each new search.

■ FOCUS and MODIFY (see Chapter 4): What's the difference? FOCUS lets you highlight terms in the documents you have already retrieved; MODIFY lets you change your original search request and search the entire file again.

Thus MODIFY can retrieve additional cases; FOCUS cannot. You can use FOCUS as many times as you like on a set of documents you have found but can use MODIFY only once, since the pool of documents will then be changed. If your original search terms appear annoyingly often, FOCUS has the advantage of letting you have only your new terms highlighted.

There is no extra search charge for using either FOCUS or MODIFY. ■

CHAPTER 5. QUICK REFERENCE PAGE

Display Modes
    .kw = KWIC
    .vk# = VAR-KWIC
    .ci = CITE
    .fu = FULL
    .se = SEGMTS

Moving within a Document
    .np = Next page
    .pp = Previous page
    .fp = First page

Moving between Documents
    .nd = Next document
    .pd = Previous document
    .fd = First document
    #   = Move to specific document #
    #.nd = Move forward # documents
    #.pd = Move back # documents

Browsing
    b   = Browse other sections of statutory or administrative
           code

Linked Documents
    .linkon = Display link markers
    .linkoff = Hide link markers

FOCUS
    .fo = FOCUS
    .ef = Exit FOCUS

6

Updating, Verifying, and Expanding Your Research

THIS CHAPTER COVERS:

On-line citators

Citation forms

Shepard's Citations

Auto-Cite

LEXCITE

LEXIS as a citator

Updating statutory research

Updating administrative codes

T HIS CHAPTER explains how to use on-line citators (Shepard's, Auto-Cite, LEXCITE, and the whole LEXIS system as a citator) to update and verify your research and to find related authorities. It also covers the use of Advance Legislative Services to update statutory materials, and Administrative Registers to update administrative codes.

On-Line Citators

A citator lists documents that cite other documents. You use a citator to find what has been said or written about a certain document. If that document is a case, statute, or regulation, a citator is used to verify that it is still "good law" and to find related law.

A citator will tell you if your case has been reversed, overruled, superseded by a statute, or otherwise invalidated and whether there are any related cases, law review articles, or other materials that cite your case. Some citators will also tell you if your citation form is correct. Reading these materials will greatly reduce your vulnerability to embarrassment and to malpractice suits.

> ■ A note for non-lawyer readers: *Bluebook: A Uniform System of Citation* is the cursed, hated, and almost universally accepted stylebook for legal citation form. You can find a copy in almost any law library or any bookstore that sells law books. It is published and distributed by the Harvard Law Review Association, Gannett House, 1511 Massachusetts Avenue, Cambridge, Massachusetts 02138. ■

Shepard's Citations is to citators what Kleenex is to tissue or Jello is to gelatin. Before on-line systems, and to a great extent today, Shepard's had such a corner on the citator market that lawyers talk about *Shepardizing* instead of *using a citator* (*citatorizing?*). When a lawyer says, "I Shepardized this case," he or she means, "I have updated my research on this case using a Shepard's citator, thus rendering myself immune to malpractice prosecution unless you count that little filing snafu."

Shepard's Citations is still the most widely used citator and is sufficient for most research purposes (it has to be, since it is all most practitioners have). In addition to Shepard's on-line, LEXIS offers Auto-Cite and LEXCITE. It is also possible to use the entire LEXIS system as a kind of do-it-yourself customized citator.

> ■ No doubt about it, come the revolution the *Bluebook* editors will be the first up against the wall, but meanwhile resistance appears to be futile. The *Bluebook* is *the* standard by which citations are judged. Fortunately, you do not have to actually *touch* a *Bluebook* to find the correct citation forms—they are available in Auto-Cite

for $4 a citation. Unless you are one of the elite few for whom the *Bluebook* holds no terror, after running a few cites in Auto-Cite you'll be begging to pay $4 a citation, at least for the tough cites. ∎

Citation Forms

Case citations must have a volume number, an abbreviated reporter name (the *Bluebook* abbreviation will always work, and sometimes other reasonable guesses will work as well), and a page number. It may occur to you that you could use Auto-Cite to see what the *Bluebook* abbreviation of your case is, except of course that you don't know the abbreviation to enter your cite in Auto-Cite in the first place. Appendix F intervenes between you and this cruel fate by listing acceptable citation forms that can be used in Auto-Cite.

LEXIS was not raised in a barn and will politely disregard any eccentricities in the way you punctuate or space the reporter abbreviation as long as you use all the letters and numbers of the correct abbreviation and put a space after the volume and before the page. Thus `1 SE2D 2`, `1 S.E.2d 2`, `1 se2d 2`, or `1 s e 2d 2` are all equally acceptable citations. It is quickest just to type your citations in lowercase letters without spaces or periods, but if this undermines your sense of consistency and order in the universe or confuses your carefully trained fingers, then by all means space and punctuate.

Shepard's Citations

Shepard's Citations gives you a list of citations of cases, ALR annotations, law review articles, and other materials that cite *your* case or statute. Shepard's on-line covers citations to state and federal cases and the statutes of the United States, Florida, Louisiana, Massachusetts, New Jersey, Ohio, and Washington. Note that the other statutes covered by the printed version of Shepard's are not available on LEXIS. It lists citing references found in state and federal cases, administrative agencies, federal law citations in law re-views, and patents. The on-line version of Shepard's does *not* cover regulations or statutes from most jurisdictions (although the printed versions do, and LEXIS plans to add more jurisdictions soon).

How Current Is It?

Cases appear in Shepard's within about 4 months of being decided.

■ In contrast to Shepard's 3- or 4-month lag time, LEXCITE can re-trieve citing cases as soon as they are available on-line (sometimes the same day they are decided, and usually within 2 weeks). ■

Oddly enough, Shepard's information is available in paper as soon as it is on-line, although of course the paper may sit on a mail truck or someone's desk for quite a while before it reaches your shelf. It is also important to be aware that Shepard's on-line version does not always go back as far as the print version. Shepard's display screens tell you what volumes are covered on-line (see "Coverage" later in this chapter) in case you are unsure of the time differences.

How to Shepardize

There are two ways to access Shepard's Service. When you want to Shepardize a document that you are viewing, type `shep` and press Enter. To use Shepard's from any other point, type `shep` followed by the citation you want to Shepardize and press Enter. For example, type `shep 101 US 1` and press Enter. Either way, the system will then display something like Figure 6.1.

Each Shepard's screen is headed "CITATIONS TO:" and the cite you entered (or the cite of the case you were viewing when you ac-cessed Shepard's). It is a good idea to check this line to make sure you are Shepardizing the case you meant to, instead of a distant typo-graphical cousin.

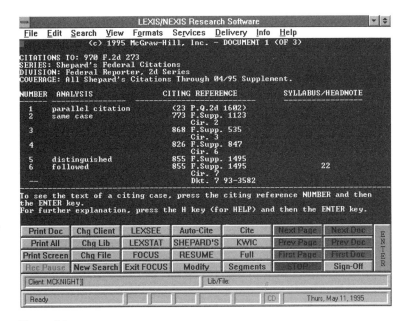

Figure 6.1

Series and Divisions

A Shepard's Citations series covers a reporter series (Southeastern Reports, for example) or a jurisdiction's statutes (say, Illinois statutes). There are also separate series for regulations, topical materials, and citations *to* law review articles (as opposed to citations *in* law review articles, which are included in state case and statute series). A division is part of a series. For example, the Federal Reporter, 2d Series, is a division of the Federal Reporter series.

When you run a citation in Shepard's you may get more than one Shepard's document. Each document shows the results retrieved from a series and division corresponding to the print version citators you would have to use in order to Shepardize your case. For example, to Shepardize an Illinois case, you would consult Shepard's Illinois Citations and Shepard's Northeastern Citations. Shepard's checks both these citators for you when you enter the regional citation. You can tell how many documents you have retrieved while on the first screen of your results by looking at the top line of the screen, which in Figure 6.1, for example, says "DOCUMENT 1 (OF 3)." Press Enter or Page Down to move through all the screens and documents of your Shepard's results. The second document of the results shown in Figure 6.1 is shown in Figure 6.2. These cross-references are retrieved for you automatically.

You do not get all the parallel citations for the citing references, but only those in the series and division that corresponds to the citation you entered. In other words, you get references to the same sort of case cite you entered; if you enter a state reporter citation, you get citations to other state reporters, not to regional reporters. If you are interested in citing references from outside your state, use the regional citation instead of the state citation to Shepardize your case.

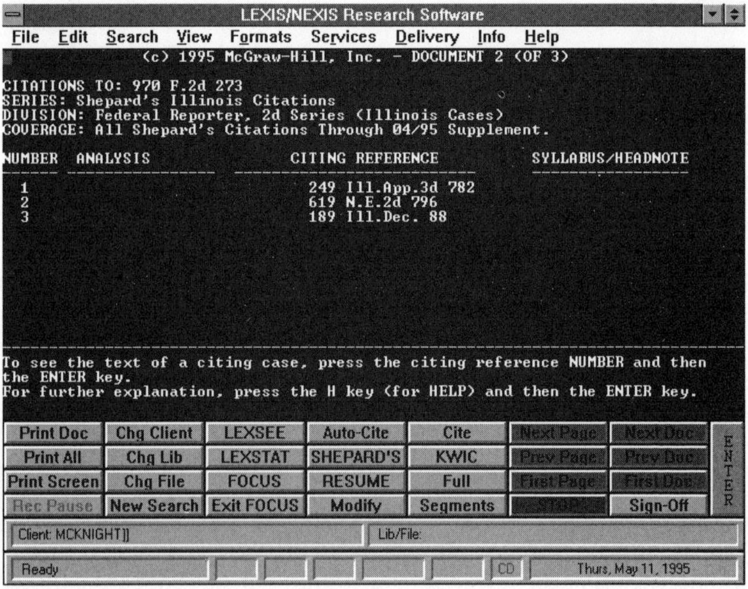

Figure 6.2

Coverage

Note that the coverage date given on the Shepard's results screen is the date of publication of the supplement covered, not the date of the latest court decisions covered, which will be 3 or 4 months earlier. In other words, everything in the 4/95 paper supplement to Shepard's was included on-line at the time Figure 6.1 was printed, but you would not expect to find citing cases that were decided more recently than 1/95 included.

To see a complete list of the sources that were checked for citing references, you have to find a print version of the citator you are using and consult the list in the front of the volume.

Number: These are the numbers by which the full text of the individual citing references can be retrieved: by entering a number you go automatically to the full text of the citing reference at the point where the reference to your case occurred. Your case citation is highlighted, making it easy to find the relevant portion of the document and evaluate the reference in context. You can page forward or back throughout the full text of the document and otherwise review it as you could any other search result (see Chapter 5). When you have perused the citing reference to your satisfaction, you can return to your Shepard's results display by entering `resume Shep`.

Citing References: A citing reference is a document that cited your case. You can pull up the text of the citing reference by entering its number (this is listed under the number column—see Figure 6.1). The screen will display the page that mentions your document first, and you can view the entire document using the usual commands for moving within a document (see Chapter 5). To return to the Shepard's screen, type `resume Shep`.

Retrieving the full text of citing references on-line is quick and easy, but of course it does cost money. You could save by printing the Shepard's screens and looking up the citations in books if you have access to them. Note that the page numbers given in the cites refer to the page where the reference appears, so you won't have to read the whole document to see what was said about your document. Because the citing references refer to the page where a reference occurs, the same document may be listed several times as a citing reference (if it refers to your case more than once, on different pages). Parallel citations and history citations are cited by the first page number, since the entire case, rather than a reference within it, is relevant.

Analysis: As you can see, there are one- or two-word analyses beside some of the citations. These explain how the citing documents are relevant to the cited document (the one you started with). For example, the analysis beside one of the case citations might say "reversed." This means that the citing case reversed *your* case, which of course is not something you want to be the last to know. If the cited case had no clear impact on your case, no analysis code is assigned to it. Here is a list of the possible analyses and their meanings.

ANALYSIS	MEANING
For Cases	
parallel citation	another place your case is printed (other than at the citation you started with)
affirmed	your case was affirmed on appeal at this cite
connected case	different case closely connected to citing case or arising out of same subject matter
dismissed	your case was dismissed on appeal
modified	your case was modified on appeal
reversed	your case was reversed on appeal at this cite
same case	same case (you're welcome)
superseded	substitution for former opinion
vacated	your case was vacated
cert den	certiorari or appeal denied or dismissed by highest state court

criticized	citing case criticizes reasoning or decision in your case
distinguished	citing case gives reasons holding in your case does not apply to it
explained	explains importance of your case
followed	citing case cites yours as controlling
harmonized	citing case explains how, even though mere mortals might think citing case flies in the face of decisions in cited case, in fact the cases are in harmony and not at odds at all
dissenting opinion	your case is cited in the dissenting opinion in this case
limited	another court refused to extend the holding in your case beyond the specific issues in your case
overruled	citing case expressly overrules yours
parallel	this means the citing case is a whole lot like yours (as in "although they now have different last names, twin sisters Abigail Van Buren and Ann Landers live parallel lives")
questioned	court in citing case just can't imagine what court in your case might have been thinking
US cert den	certiorari denied by US Supreme Court
US cert dis	certiorari dismissed by US Supreme Court
US reh den	rehearing denied by US Supreme Court
US reh dis	rehearing dismissed by US Supreme Court

For Statutes

The following notations simply identify a form of statute:

amendment

appendix

article

chapter

clause

division

executive order

extra session

House bill

House resolution

joint resolution

number

page

paragraph

part

part resolution

private law

proclamation

public law

section

statutes at large

subchapter

subclause

subdivision

subparagraph

subsection

veterans' regulations

The following describe the operation of a statute.

TERM	EXPLANATION
amended	this statute amended yours
added	new section added to existing statute
extended	part of statute extended to apply to later statute, or time allowed by statute for performance of duties is extended
limited	statute declared not to be extended to apply to later statute
repealed	statute is no more
reenacted	statute died but was reincarnated as this new (yet really just the same) statute
renumbered	same statute, new numbering scheme
repealed in part	part of statute is no more, other part lives on, sadder but wiser
repealed and superseded	statute has been replaced by new statute
revised	statute has been changed
superseded	replaces old legislation which is not expressly done in
superseded in part	superseded, in part (you're welcome again)
suspended	statute must sit on bench until further notice
suspended in part	part of statute must sit on bench until further notice
supplementing	added to existing statute
unconstitutional	conflicts with Constitution and is thus void
valid, validated	statute noted as rightful
void or invalid	statute is not good law (may be against public policy or in conflict with higher law, for example), has no force

Syllabus/Headnote: The numbers in this column correspond to the headnote numbers in the cited case. If a syllabus/headnote number is given, it means that the citing reference addresses the issue that is summarized in that headnote number *in the cited case.* In other words, if a citing reference has a "3" beside it under the syllabus/headnote heading, that citing reference addresses the issue that is summarized in headnote 3 of the cited case. See Figures 6.3 and 6.4. Note that Figure 6.4 is a page of a case from a West® Reporter, showing West's headnote numbers, which are not available on LEXIS. Thus you can use Shepard's on-line to see what cases cite a West case for a principal in one of its headnotes, but you can't see what the headnote actually says unless you have access to a copy of the West case including West's headnotes. These are available on Westlaw, LEXIS's competitor, or in print and CD-ROM versions of West reporters.

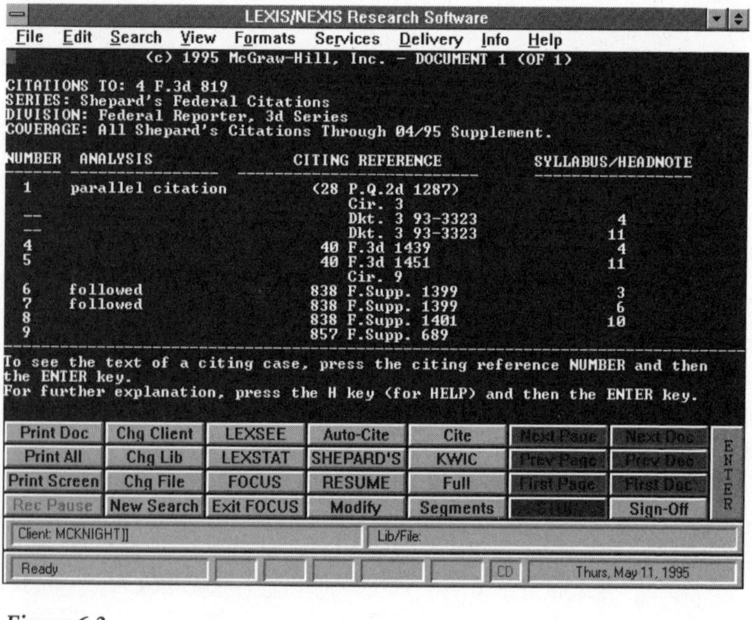

Figure 6.3

Reviewing Your Shepard's Results

To review your Shepard's results, use Next Page, Previous Page, Next Document, and so on, as explained in the chapter on looking at what you've found (Chapter 5).

Shepardizing Another Case or Statute

Once you are on a Shepard's screen, you can shepardize another case by typing the citation and pressing Enter. This is *much* cheaper than returning to a database and pulling up the case to Shepardize it.

Limiting Your Shepard's Results

If you want to look for a certain kind of case treatment or history (say, cases that explained yours), you can enter the abbreviation of the sort of treatment or history you want. For example, if you want to see only explaining cases, type e and press Enter. Shepard's will display a list of cases that have explained your case. If you aren't sure what your choices are, type . se and press Enter to see what types you have to choose from in the series and division you are in and select one or more. The system will then display only the types of cases you have requested. To go back to the full Shepard's listing, type . fu and press Enter.

Using Shepard's to Find Related Cases

By Shepardizing a case on a point, you can find related cases, since they are likely to cite your case. This can be a way to find materials that evade you through index searches. If you are looking for materials that deal with an isolated issue in your case and you have a print version with headnotes, you can pick out the citations that list that issue's headnote number. See the section on syllabus and headnote numbers earlier in this chapter. Note that headnote numbers refer to different issues in each case, so that you cannot know what issue a numbered headnote deals with in a particular case unless you read it. Headnotes are not included in cases on-line in LEXIS, so you can make use of them only if you have access to the print version of the case or another source such as Westlaw (this is one of the few significant differences between Westlaw and LEXIS).

Getting Out of Shepard's

To get out of Shepard's and back to where you were, type `.es` and press Enter or type `resume` and press Enter. You can return to a particular service by typing `resume` and the name of the service—for example, `resume LEXIS` or `resume LEXCITE`.

If you have used multiple services before you type `resume`, the system will display a Resume Options screen, which is its way of asking "resume what?" Follow the directions on the screen to return to the setting of your choice.

Shepard's On-Line versus Shepard's Print Versions

Advantages of Shepard's on-line over Shepard's on paper:

- ◆ You can use it without memorizing or looking up all those pesky little abbreviations.

- ◆ You can view the full text of the citing document with one keystroke.

- ◆ The supplements are never missing, and you get the information from all of them automatically instead of having to look up your citation three or more times.

- ◆ You never have to leave your chair.

Disadvantages:

- ◆ Maybe you *like* to leave your chair now and then.

- ◆ Four dollars a cite. Every cite. Of course, the books are not free either, but if you are buying them anyway this is extra expense for each search.

♦ Carpal tunnel syndrome.

♦ If you are single, there goes your chance for a serendipitous meeting in the citator section of your local law library. Still, there's always the frozen-entrees-for-one section at the Piggly-Wiggly.

LEXIS would love for you to do all your Shepardizing on-line, at $4 a cite, but you can use the paper versions of Shepard's all or some of the time if you prefer. They are, oddly enough, just as up-to-date as the on-line versions, presuming you have no low-life Shepard's hoarders in your law library. If you want more current info, you need to go with LEXCITE or LEXIS as a citator—more on this later.

Auto-Cite

Auto-Cite is LEXIS's citation verification service. When you give it a citation to any state or federal case, it gives you

♦ The name of the case

♦ The official citation of the case in *Bluebook* format

♦ The year the case was decided

♦ The jurisdiction of the court

♦ Parallel citations in *Bluebook* format

♦ Cases that have cited your case *and affected or validated* its precedential value

♦ Appellate history of the case (what happened with the same parties in the same dispute before or after your case)

♦ A list of citations of cases to which your case makes negative reference

♦ A list of ALR annotation and LE2d articles that have cited your case

■ Auto-Cite's coverage is significantly different from Shepard's Citations.

  ♦ Shepard's gives you all the cases that cite your case. Auto-Cite gives *only* the ones that affect its precedential value. Thus Auto-Cite is useful for determining whether your case is still good law but not for finding all the cases that have anything to say about your case.

  ♦ Auto-Cite also gives you names and citations to ALR annotations. Shepard's only gives citations.

  ♦ Auto-Cite gives you the correct *Bluebook* citation to your case, including date and jurisdiction. Shepard's does not.

  ♦ Auto-Cite gives the complete appellate history of your case; what happened with the same dispute before and after your case (appeals and original cases of which your case is an appeal). Shepard's lists only cases that cited your case, which excludes cases it was appealed from, by definition.

  ♦ Auto-Cite lists cases *upon which* your case has had a negative impact. Shepard's does not: it gives only cases that cited your case.

  ♦ Auto-Cite runs about 1 to 4 weeks behind the courts; Shepard's runs about 3 to 4 months behind them. ■

Non-Case Citations: In addition to cites to cases, Auto-Cite verifies cites to IRS Revenue Rulings and Revenue Procedures and cites from many looseleaf reporters (such as CCH Reporters), administrative law, ALR annotations, and LE2d articles). The GUIDE library contains a listing of Auto-Citeable (well, if it isn't a word, it should be) documents and their abbreviations, reprinted in Appendix F.

Coverage Dates: Auto-Cite covers LEXIS cites from 1988. Citing cases appear within about 1 to 4 weeks of being decided.

How to Use Auto-Cite

To use Auto-Cite while viewing a document, type ac and press Enter. To Auto-Cite a document you are viewing, enter ac. To Auto-

Cite a document you are not viewing, type ac followed by a space and the citation and press Enter. The first screen of your Auto-Cite results will be displayed (the upper right-hand corner tells you how many screens there are). Auto-Cite displays differ depending on the results retrieved but may include the following elements (see Figures 6.4A through 6.4E):

1. Citation you entered. Well, not quite. This heading should really read "correct *Bluebook* form for the citation you entered." This shows the citation for your case in correct *Bluebook* form, complete with correctly abbreviated, punctuated, and spaced names, date, jurisdiction, and parallel cites. This may save you having to look up the case itself and Shepardize it, or worse, having to use the *Bluebook* (if this book had a soundtrack, ominous music would play each time the *Bluebook* was mentioned; if you've had much contact with the *Bluebook* you are probably supplying the ominous music yourself).

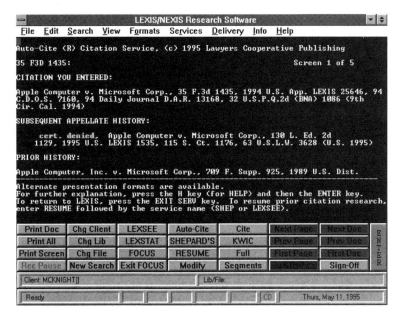

Figure 6.4A

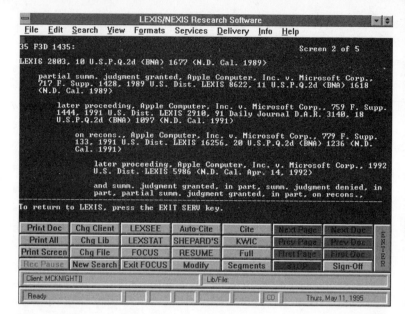

Figure 6.4B

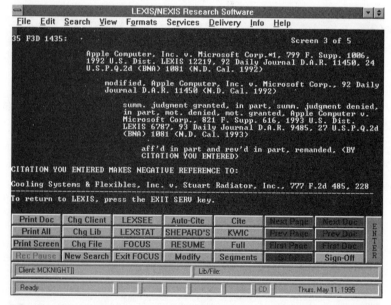

Figure 6.4C

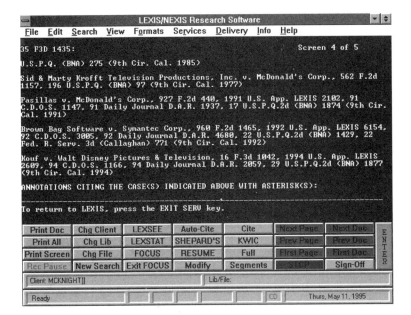

Figure 6.4D

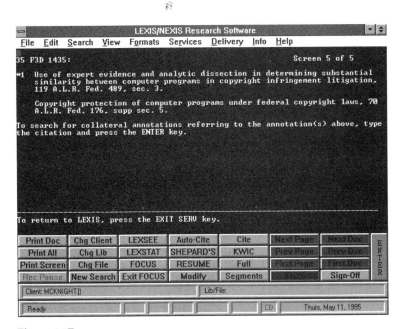

Figure 6.4E

2. Subsequent appellate history. This lists any developments in your case since the decision you started with. For example, if your case has been reversed, you'll hear about it here.

3. Subsequent treatment history. This lists cases that cite yours negatively. In other words, if you are Auto-Citing the "Smith" case, you'll get cases that overruled, disapproved, criticized, or didn't follow your case (or "criticized but reluctantly followed by"). This heading also lists conflicting authorities noted in your case itself, and superseding statutes.

4. Prior history. Citations to published actions that happened in your case before the opinion you started with. For example, the intermediate appellate court opinion of your Supreme Court case.

5. Annotations. ALR annotations that cite your case *or* a case listed under subsequent treatment history for your case are listed by title and citation. The titles can help you identify the most useful annotations. This is a slight improvement over Shepard's results display of ALR annotations, which lists only the citations. The ALR annotations list is broken up into separate lists for each cited case, headed by an asterisk and a number that corresponds to the number under the ALR annotations heading where a list of annotations citing each particular case can be found.

To Auto-Cite Another Case

$ To Auto-Cite another case while on an Auto-Cite screen, type its citation. This is much less expensive than exiting Auto-Cite to go to the case itself and running another Auto-Cite from there.

■ When to use Shepard's and when to use Auto-Cite:

Use Auto-Cite when you need
A full citation in correct *Bluebook* form
The titles of relevant ALR annotations

> The complete appellate history of your case (cases it was an appeal of and appeals of it)
>
> Use Shepard's Citations when you need
> *All* cases that cited your case ∎

To exit Auto-Cite (and you must exit Auto-Cite to do anything else) type `resume` or `.es` and press Enter. If you have used multiple services before you type `resume`, the system will display a Resume Options screen, which is its way of saying "resume what?" To choose a resume option, type = and the number beside the desired option and press Enter.

LEXCITE

LEXCITE finds documents (in the specific library and file that you select) that cite your document. You can use LEXCITE in files containing cases, law review articles, agency decisions, federal register pages, ALR annotations, comptroller general decisions, or American maritime cases. You cannot use it for statutes or administrative materials, although you can achieve the same effect through a slightly different route (see the section in this chapter on using LEXIS as a citator).

LEXCITE will retrieve more current documents than Shepard's Citations can, and it is not limited to any particular reporter system (although it is, of course, limited to documents included in the LEXIS database).

LEXCITE doesn't give editorial labels the way Shepard's does. It just gives you the citing documents themselves, as if to say, "Here is everything, even the really new stuff, but I haven't had any time to look at it yet, so *you* sort it out." This isn't as convenient as the ready-labeled information in Shepard's and Auto-Cite, but you don't have to read all the documents through to pick out the important stuff. You can view the documents in KWIC to go directly to the part that cites your document so you can see what was written and in what context.

How Current Is LEXCITE?

LEXCITE will find the most current cases that cite your case. A citing case may appear through LEXCITE as many as four months before it appears in Shepard's.

How to Use LEXCITE

To use LEXCITE, you must first select a library and file (unlike Shepard's and Auto-Cite, which you can use from the menu screen or anywhere else). Then type LEXCITE followed by a space and your citation and press Enter.

The system displays LEXCITE results the same way it displays other search results; instead of a special "table" screen like Shepard's and Auto-Cite, it displays the documents themselves, in KWIC format unless you specify otherwise (by typing .fu for full, .ci for a list of citations, and so on; see Chapter 5 for more information on display formats). The citation for which you searched and the names of the parties to the case are highlighted in the text of the retrieved documents.

Getting Out of LEXCITE

To exit LEXCITE (and you must exit LEXCITE to do anything else), type resume or .es and press Enter. If you have used multiple services before you type resume, the system will display a Resume Options screen. Follow the directions on the screen to return to whatever you would like.

LEXCITE versus LEXSTAT or LEXSEE

Note that, although LEXSTAT and LEXSEE sound a lot like LEXCITE, they do not do the same sort of thing at all. LEXSEE and LEXSTAT let you see only the text of the document cite you enter. LEXCITE retrieves documents that cited your document; LEXSTAT and LEXSEE find only the document itself. So if you LEXCITE a case (by entering `LEXCITE` and the case cite), you get all the documents that cited that case, but if you LEXSEE a case (by entering `LEXSEE` and the cite), you get only the text of the case itself.

Which Citator Should I Use?

It depends (isn't that always the way? You want a simple answer just once . . .). Shepard's gives you thorough citation information all predigested and flagged for important stuff. For more current references, you'll have to use LEXCITE or Auto-Cite. Which one? Well . . . that's right, it depends. LEXCITE has the most current and complete references and it lets you customize your search to deal with a specific issue, but it can also give you an awful lot to read through with no editorial assist and is usually the most expensive citator to use. Auto-Cite cuts out a lot of reading and decision making, giving you only the correct *Bluebook* form of your cite, the cases that affect the precedential value of your case, and earlier cases upon which your case had a negative impact. This brevity is both the good thing about Auto-Cite and also the bad. If you have to be in court in three minutes with a case you just found, Auto-Cite is the way to go. If you want to see everything ever written about your document, use LEXCITE.

   If your document isn't covered by the citators, use LEXIS itself as a citator.

Using LEXIS as a Citator

Using LEXIS as a citator simply means that you run a search in a library and file of your choice for terms and connectors that identify your document. You might search for the citation of the document, the title, or some other distinguishing element. One of the special abilities of LEXIS as a citator versus the citator services (Shepard's, Auto-Cite, and LEXCITE) is that you can search by elements or combinations of elements other than the citation. Suppose, for example, that you are only interested in citations to documents that mention your case in a specific context. With LEXIS as a citator you can combine a subject and citation ("67 us 321 and damages," for example) to do just this.

LEXIS as a citator is also especially useful for tracking citations to statutes and administrative materials (other than the federal register) that are not accessible through LEXCITE. LEXCITE is just an automated (and less expensive) way to use LEXIS as a citator for selected documents. You'll want to use LEXCITE instead of LEXIS as a citator whenever possible, since it costs $4 a citation instead of $24 to $95 for a search charge. Another big advantage of LEXCITE is that it finds parallel citations and spacing or punctuation variations automatically. With LEXIS as a citator, you have to use a character-for-character citation ("42 N.E.2d 210," for example, which won't find 42 NE2d 210 or other variations that may appear) or a connector that is likely to be over inclusive ("42 PRE/5 210" could get a lot of things other than 42 N.E.2d 210).

■ The *big* downside to using LEXIS as a citator is cost: it costs the same to use LEXIS as a citator as to run any other search in a file ($24 to $95). Shepard's, Auto-Cite, and LEXCITE cost (at the risk of sounding like a broken record) $4. ■

Search Queries with LEXIS

Remember that you must first select an appropriate library and file. You may then search for citations to your document using a query formulated according to the usual rules (see Chapter 3).

A numerical citation works well, but use LEXCITE instead unless the citation is to a statute or another document not available through LEXCITE. Section symbols often cause problems in citations; they are best left out of searches. Usually the best way to search for a statutory cite is to look for the numbers (title and section, for example, as in 29 U.S.C. 1983) within five or so terms of each other ("29 W/5 1983"). This picks up references to section 1983 of title 29 or the other way around, and most other reasonable variations as well. The same approach works well for administrative regulations, although it is safer to include "cfr" in the search rather than "usc," since there are no real alternatives (such as U.S.C.A. or U.S.C.S.). Something like "33 W/5 cfr W/5 210.32" will pick up a lot of variations.

One thing to keep in mind with section numbers is that they may end in a smaller number or a different letter than the one you have searched for. Section 242.31(a) might interest you, but you'll miss it if you search for "242." The computer reads *242.3* as a term different from *242*, just as it reads *office* as a word different from *officer*. This is just as well if you don't want to see citations to subparts of your cited statute. If you want to avoid this effect, you can end a section number with an exclamation point to retrieve that number even with other additional numbers or letters tacked on to it. (Thus you would type 242 ! to retrieve 242, 242.3, and 242.31(a).) See Chapter 3 for more information on the use of the exclamation point to retrieve varied endings.

Constitutions pose special problems because they are sometimes cited with roman numerals (I, II, and III) or ordinal numbers (1st, 2nd, and 3rd). To search for references to the first amendment, you'll need to search for "amendment W/5 (first OR 1st or 1 or i)" to pick up all the possible variations.

A numerical citation to a statute (29 U.S.C. sec. 1983) may miss some variations of spacings and punctuation or even the code version (U.S.C.A., for example). You can retrieve more possible variations (doubtless including some to other documents that you do not want) by using PRE/5 as a connector. You could use a number other than 5 if the citation seems to warrant it.

To search by a case name, avoid specifying the entire name if it is long, since this will miss all the shortened references that are likely to occur. Rather than search for Ms. Elizabeth Susan Zerbert v. Big

Roscoe's All-You-Can-Eat Cinnamon Bun and Catfish Emporium, pick a few of the more unusual terms to search with ("Zerbert AND catfish emporium" should do it). Try to pick the terms that bring the phrase, "How many can there possibly be?" to mind. When using the PRE/# connector, keep in mind that the parties in some cases take up nearly a whole page. If you have no idea how long the full name of the case is, it is better to start with a high number and modify downward to reduce false hits as you discover them. If you start too low, you may miss relevant documents or have to do (and pay for) a new search (see Chapter 4). On the other hand, a very long name is almost certain to be shortened by any writer for readability's sake, so PRE/15 is probably a good starting point.

Add any limitations you like to your search query. You could add a segment or date limitation (as in "42 us 210 AND date aft 1990"; see Chapter 4 for more explanation of date and segment searching) or a topic with any number of terms and connectors (as in "38 N.E.2d 222 AND res ipsa loquitur").

When searching for secondary materials such as law review articles or treatises, use the more unusual words in the title or author names. "Corbin W/5 contracts" is better than "Corbin's text on contracts" because it allows for many more variations in citation. Most lawyers are familiar with *Corbin on Contracts*, but how many could tell you that the correct title is *Corbin's Text on Contracts?*

Using LEXIS as a citator lets you find citations to documents not covered by the citator services, using searches as varied as you care to make them. Try to think of all the ways a harried author might have cited your document at 3 A.M., and plan your searches accordingly.

Updating Statutes

The various CODES files are only as up-to-date as the printed codes they are based on (well, a little more up-to-date, depending on printing and mailing lags), so you need to update on-line code research with a legislative service just as you would with print code research. There is an advance legislative service on-line for each state and a PUBLAW file (equivalent to the state advance legislative services) for federal statutes, so this is fairly easy to do, and it will yield more current information than a print legislative service.

For each state, the Advance Legislative Service file is called XXALS (substitute the two-letter state postal code for the XX) in the CODES library. The federal equivalent is the PUBLAW file, also in the CODES library. These files have session laws (laws as soon as they are passed, before they have even had time to be added to the code) of that state or the United States. Session laws usually appear on-line within about a week of passage.

You can use these files to update your code research by searching for applicable code sections and subjects. For example, you could search for 42 uscs 12101 in the PUBLAW file to see if it has been repealed, amended, or otherwise referred to in the session laws. You can also search for mentions of the subject you are researching to see if there is any new relevant legislation.

Currency

Federal and most state session laws are available on-line in the PUBLAW file within 10 working days after they are passed. You can check to see how up-to-date a particular Advance Legislative Service is on a particular day by searching for documents added after a given date (2 weeks ago would be a safe place to start) and checking the resulting citation list to see when the most recent bill listed was passed. Bills are listed in reverse chronological order, so the first one listed is the newest. Such a search would read something like "date after 9/4/95." Updating lags are not likely to be totally consistent from day to day, but they don't tend to vary by more than a few days. Note that checking this by doing searches is expensive if you are paying by the search; you might want to use the 800 number instead if you need a precise coverage date on a given occasion.

Legislation Still in the Legislature

Bill tracking (summaries of pending bills) and bill text (text of pending bills) files are available for all states and the U.S. Congress.

In the CODES library, there is an XXTRCK for each state (again, substitute the state's two-letter postal abbreviation for the XX). For each bill pending in the legislature, this file has a document that summarizes the bill, who or what the bill would affect, and where it currently is in the legislative process ("passed house," for example).

Bill tracking includes all bills considered in the current legislative session. If the bill was introduced in the current session and has already been passed, it will say "became Public Law" and the Public Law citation will be in the Final Status segment.

Bill text files consist of the full text of pending bills. In some states (currently these are California, Colorado, Delaware, Florida, Illinois, Massachusetts, Michigan, New Jersey, Ohio, Pennsylvania, Texas, and Wisconsin—but check this, it's changing fast), there is an XXTEXT file (substitute the state's postal code for the XX) in the CODES library that has the full text of every pending bill. The federal bill text file is BLTEXT, also in the CODES library.

■ A CONGRESSIONAL DATABASE FOR BOOKIES
BLCAST gives the probability that a given federal bill will pass as guessed (excuse me, *estimated*) by the staff of Information for Public Affairs, Inc. Consider starting a new office pool (loser pays next month's LEXIS bill?). This file is not available for states. ■

Updating Administrative Codes

You can update your research in the Code of Federal Regulations by searching for the subject in question and any applicable CFR sections in the Federal Register database. This will find any new regulations on your subject or any that affect your CFR section explicitly.

Most state administrative codes and registers are not available on LEXIS at the time of this writing, but there are plans to add them soon, so check your alphabetical list or menu screens to see if a state of interest to you has been added. If the state has a code and register, the same strategy as you use for the federal register will work there.

In addition to checking available registers to update your administrative code section, you can search case or secondary material files to see if the section has been cited there, thus possibly finding helpful interpretive materials. You can't do this in print research at this time since there are no print citators that assume this function for state administrative materials.

When you search for administrative code sections, remember to allow for variations in citation forms by using title and section numbers with connectors and the code title (and universal characters if you want any possible subsections—see Chapter 3), rather than typing in a "correct" citation. An example of a broadly inclusive CFR section search would be "cfr W/10 29 W/10 340!" The exclamation point picks up your section despite any additional numbers or letters attached to it (340.345a, for example).

CHAPTER 6.   QUICK REFERENCE PAGE

| | USE TO FIND | |
	FUNCTION	CURRENCY
Shepard's	Retrieves analyzed citing documents	Same as printed version of Shepard's—3–4 months behind courts.
Auto-Cite	Gives correct *Bluebook* cite, appellate history of your case, cases that had a negative impact on your case's value as precedent, cases your case had a negative impact on, and ALR citations	Varies. Direct history is available within 4 days (often just hours), indirect is 2–61 weeks behind the courts.
Using LEXIS as a citator	Retrieves unanalyzed citing documents	Retrieves the most current information available on LEXIS
LEXCITE (LEXIS as a citator automated for cases)	Retrieves unanalyzed citing documents—searches for parallel cites automatically	Retrieves the most current information available on LEXIS

CHAPTER 6.   QUICK REFERENCE PAGE

	USE TO FIND
CITES TO	TO USE
Cases, decisions of selected administrative agencies. NOT statutes or regulations.	When viewing case, type `shep`. To Shepardize cite, type `shep` and cite (example: `shep 101 US 1`)
Cases only	When viewing case, type `ac`. To Auto-Cite cite, type `ac` and cite (example: `ac 101 US 1`)
Non-case materials	Select library and file, search for cite using connectors. Can be limited to cites dealing with specific issue by adding terms to search (example: "501 PRE/5 1281 and covenant")
Cases, ALR, U.S. Code, law reviews, federal register, comptroller general opinions	Select library and file, search for cite using connectors. Can be limited to cites dealing with specific issue by adding terms to search (example: "501 PRE/5 1281 and covenant")

Note that Shepard's and Auto-Cite cost $4 a search, while LEXIS as a citator and LEXCITE cost $24 to $95 per search, depending on which file you select.

7

Printing or Storing Searches and Results

THIS CHAPTER COVERS:

Hardware options

Having LEXIS print and mail your document

The print commands

"Printing" to a disk (downloading or storing on disk)

Printing from a disk

Keeping records of your research

Session Recording

LOG

Prettifying what you print

Costs

Documents retrieved through LEXIS or NEXIS can easily be stored and retrieved for future use. You can print a screen while you are viewing it, tell your computer to print or store entire documents after you sign off, or even have LEXIS print them and mail them to you. You can also keep track of the searches you've run by using the session-recording feature to record every screen you look at or by using the LOG feature to record each search query, library, and file used. Keeping records of what you've done helps prevent duplication of efforts and costs and helps you . . . well, keep good records.

121

Hardware Options

You may print using either an attached or a stand-alone printer, or have LEXIS print documents in Dayton and mail them to you. Which of these options are available to you depends on your subscription agreement with LEXIS.

An Attached Printer

You may use a printer attached to your PC to print the documents you want. This is the simplest solution to printing needs, but your PC will be tied up with "supervising" while your attached printer is printing, so you won't be able to do more searches, or word process your daily letter to Elvis, or play mine-sweeper until you are through. You ordinarily select documents to be printed while you search, and the computer saves them up to print off-line after you have signed off. Printer prices have dropped significantly in recent years and print quality has improved, making it increasingly feasible and desirable to have your own printer.

A Stand-Alone Printer

An alternative to the attached printer is a dedicated printer with its own phone line to LEXIS. By "dedicated," I mean that this printer's sole purpose is to print LEXIS and NEXIS documents. It is not attached to your PC and does nothing except sit by its phone line and wait to print something when LEXIS calls and says it is needed. Thus you can print without tying up your computer. Perhaps not coincidentally, this type of printer is called a SAP (stand-alone printer). It can also allow multiple LEXIS users, who may or may not be at the same location, to share a single printer.

"Printing" to a Disk

Instead of printing documents on paper, you can "print" them to a disk (this is known as *downloading* among the chic computer-speak set). LEXIS charges just as much to print to disk as to paper ($2 a document), but you save the cost of paper, ink, and printer wear and tear, and you conserve space in your briefcase or file cabinet. It is also a little quicker to download than to print, and it's quieter (how much quieter depends on how fast and quiet your printer is). If you have to share a printer with other people in your home or office and you need to use it for other things besides LEXIS, this is the ticket for you. You just download ("print") what you want to the disk, and later, at your leisure, you carry the disk to the printer down the hall or to your uncle Bob's and print out what you want. If you are adept at editing with DOS or a word-processing program, you can eliminate those sometimes useless pages of information at the beginning and end of the file, thereby saving paper when you do print. You can also download to a disk when you are working away from your office on your laptop, and print from the disk later.

Having LEXIS Print and Mail Your Document

An option for those lonely souls who still have no printer to call their own is to have documents printed in Dayton and mailed by next-day air. Obviously this takes time and is not inexpensive either. Take a good look at the new printer prices before you decide to take this stone-age route. One good use for this service might be to have documents printed and mailed to third parties who need them without the hassle of printing and making a trip to the post office yourself. Note that this option is not available to most law students as part of the law-school user package.

The Print Commands

You can print a screen or document you are viewing or all or selected documents retrieved by your current search. Printing a screen is free, except of course for paper, ink, and printer cost and any connect time charges. Printing documents or a citation list costs $2 per document, whether you print to paper or a disk.

To Print a Screen

The Print Screen command prints only the screen you are viewing at the time you issue the command. Some printers will not print out a single screen until you take them off-line (press the On-Line/Off-Line button or whatever looks closest) and press the form feed button on the printer. Printing a screen is actually controlled by your operating system (DOS, for example), rather than your LEXIS software, so commands vary slightly as follows:

DOS Users: Press the Shift and Print Screen keys to print (or just the Print Screen key if you are using a LEXIS 2000 or IBM ps/2 keyboard). Your particular Print Screen key may be labeled Print Screen, Prtsc, or just Print.

Windows Users: Click on the Print Screen button on your screen (near the bottom left-hand corner of the screen). This causes the text of your screen to print. You can also get a "picture" of the screen into the Windows clipboard by pressing the Print Screen key on your keyboard, and later pasting the screen into a word-processed document (see your Windows manual).

Mac Users: Press the Open Apple, Shift, and number 4 keys simultaneously. Alternatively, select Print from the menu, and then select Print Screen.

To Print a Document You Are Viewing

Print Doc prints the entire document you are viewing, not just the screen you are viewing. Enter .pr. A screen like the one shown in Figure 7.1 will appear.

After you choose a document delivery option, you will be prompted to confirm your order (see Figure 7.2).

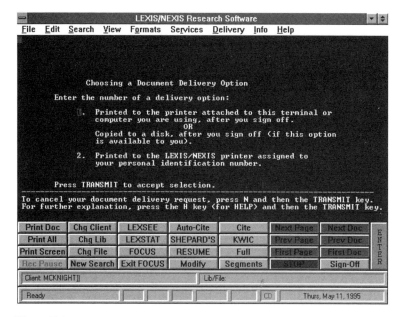

Figure 7.1

Your document will be printed in the full-text format unless you select another format at this point (select CITE by entering `.ci` or KWIC by entering `.kw`). Your destination will depend on the printing options in your subscription agreement.

If you confirm your order, it will print to the attached printer or disk *after you sign off* unless you send it to a stand-alone printer, in which case it will begin printing as soon as it reaches the front of the printing queue—as soon as the printer is done printing orders it received before yours. If you cancel, it won't print—ever. Either way, press Enter to go back to the document.

When you sign off, LEXIS will ask whether you want any documents you ordered to print on the attached printer or to disk (see "Printing from a Disk" later in this chapter). Any print requests you made during your research session will be printed or saved to disk together; you can't print some of them on paper and some to a disk. If

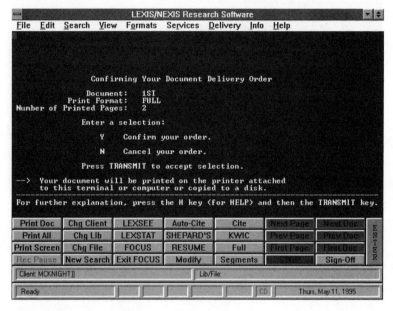

Figure 7.2

you want to print to a disk, you must choose a disk drive and file name (see "Printing" to a Disk at the end of this section on print commands).

To Print Retrieved Documents

Print All prints all the documents retrieved by your current search or selected documents specified by you. Enter .pa to print all. You will be prompted to select a location for printing or storing (see Figure 7.3).

After you select your print or storage destination, another screen asks you to confirm or cancel and gives you a chance to select specific documents (see Figure 7.4).

If you choose to print only selected documents, the system will display a menu of selections options (see Figure 7.5).

Note that you can select a single document by typing its number (if you don't know its number, go back and look at the cite list by

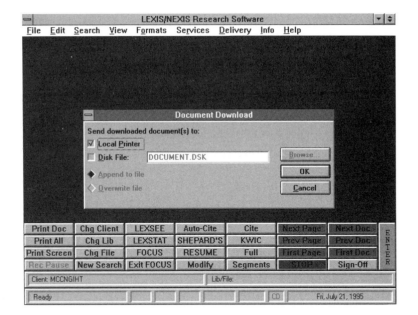

Figure 7.3

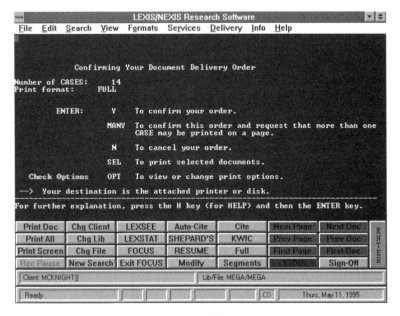

Figure 7.4

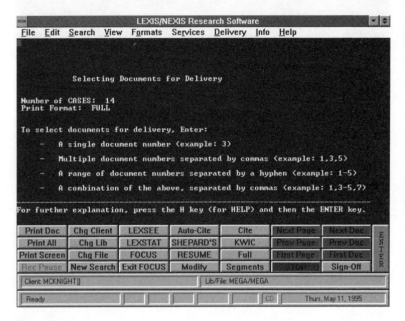

Figure 7.5

canceling your print request, pressing Enter, and then typing `.ci`). You can order several documents by typing individual document numbers with commas between them (`2, 4, 6, 8`), a range of numbers (`1-5`), or a combination (`2, 4, 6-9`). If you don't select specific documents, all the documents retrieved by your current search will be printed or stored. You will be asked to confirm your selected document delivery order (see Figure 7.6).

Check the print format and selected document numbers for errors, since this is your last chance to correct the order. If you confirm your order, just as it prints a document you are viewing, LEXIS will print to the attached printer or disk *after you sign off* unless you send it to the stand-alone printer, in which case it will begin printing as soon as it reaches the front of the printing queue. If you cancel, it won't print—ever. Either way, press Enter to go back to the document.

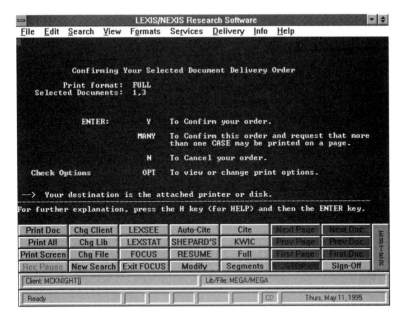

Figure 7.6

When you sign off, LEXIS will ask whether you want the document to print on the attached printer or to disk. If you want it to print to disk, you must specify a disk and file name and, of course, remember to put a disk in the correct drive if you aren't saving to your hard drive.

To Have Documents Printed in Dayton and Mailed

Use `.mi` instead of `.pr`. Note that this option is not available to law students or others who have not subscribed to the print and mail service. Contact your LEXIS representative to have this service added to your subscription. As you might suspect, this is not a free service. Evaluate carefully the time and money costs of this method versus buying your own printer, keeping in mind that you can probably use a printer for other office operations or for letters to your favorite soap opera star.

"Printing" to a Disk (Downloading or Storing on Disk)

To store your document(s) to disk, you must enter a path and file name where you want it to go (screen). If you don't specify one, it will be stored as DOCUMENT.DSK in the directory with your LEXIS software (often C:\LEXIS for DOS systems, C:\WINDOWS\LEXIS for Windows systems). If the file you name already exists, you must specify whether you want to append your document to it (keeping what is already in there intact), replace it, or change its name.

Printing from a Disk

Once you have stored documents on a disk (either by "printing" them to your disk or by using the Session Record feature), you can print them by using the PRINTSES utility that is included with your Mead Data Central communications software (yeses, that's rightses, PRINTSES). To use the PRINTSES utility, type `PRINTSES` and the name of the disk and file you want to print: `PRINTSES B:mydoc.dsk,` for example.

Documents are stored on disk in ASCII text files, so if you are the sort of technical guru to whom that means something, you can get to it with your word processor or Nintendo or whatever strikes your fancy. Such antics are beyond the scope of this book, but your LEXIS representative may be able to advise you.

Keeping Records of Your Research

Session Recording

Press the Alt and F2 keys (or Shift and F11 if you are using a LEXIS 2000 or IBM ps/2 keyboard). You will be prompted to enter a drive and file name. Be sure you have a disk in the drive you specify if you aren't using the hard drive. Type in the drive you want to use and a file name (up to eight characters) and press Enter. Each screen you view will be stored automatically from this point on until you turn it off by pressing Alt and F2 (or Shift and F1 on the LEXIS 2000 keyboard) again.

LOG

LOG saves a record of your search request, the library and file searched, and the number of documents retrieved. To use LOG, just type .keep while on your results screen. LEXSEE, LEXSTAT, Shepard's, and Auto-Cite searches are automatically saved. LOG will hold up to 999 searches a day.

To review searches saved in LOG, type .log. You can return to the logged search results by moving your cursor to the number in front of the desired LOG record and pressing Enter or by typing an equal sign followed by the number identifying that LOG search (type =2 to return to the results of the second search in LOG). When you return to search results from LOG, the LOG record of those results is deleted automatically, so you'll have to save them again if you want them to stay in the log. Remember that LOG results are deleted automatically at the end of the period you specify when you sign off, so if you want a permanent record of them, you'll have to print them or store them to a disk. To delete the LOG record you are viewing, type .del, or delete everything in the day's log with one fell swoop with .deall.

Prettifying What You Print

If you have a laser printer, you can use dual-column printing to make your cases look like cases in reporters rather than LEXIS screens. Dual-column print formats your document into two columns (just the sort of keen analytical observation you were hoping for) with footnotes at the bottom if there are any.

If you are using LEXIS for DOS or Windows, there is a Jurisoft program called LEXFORM that you can use to make your printouts from a disk more attractive and readable. Without LEXFORM, printed LEXIS documents are broken up by the headers for every screen, and they are often oddly formatted because each line on the LEXIS screen has a hard return after it.

There is no equivalent of LEXFORM for the Mac. Without LEXFORM, the best you can do to get rid of all those headers and re-turns is to use the search and replace feature of your word-processing system. If you take out all the returns, you won't have any paragraph breaks at all. To avoid this, search for all the returns with an indent or tab right after them (usually the end of one paragraph and the start of another), and convert all of these to some code term (such as "jellybeans" or "Elvis lives"). Then you can take out all the returns, re-replace the code term with a return and tab, and voila, you've got paragraphs. It would probably be prudent to keep the code terms clean in case you make a mistake—I can imagine an ugly scenario involving late-night printings being passed along to the se-nior partner without the code terms ("senior partner is a potato head"?) having been replaced.

If all of this turns your mind to mush, you have three alterna-tives: 1) buy an IBM-compatible PC and give your Mac to the kids to play their Disney programs on (No kids? A little potting soil, a gera-nium or two, and a single, well-placed kick and your Mac can be-come a lovely, decorative planter); 2) Write Jurisoft and ask them to come up with a Mac version of LEXFORM; or 3) leave the headers and returns in and get on with your life.

Costs

To recap the cost considerations mentioned in this chapter: printing a screen is "free" (you pay only for the time it takes to print the screen while you are on-line (if you are billed for connect time). Printing or downloading off-line costs $2 a document. Downloading documents to a disk lets you store them quickly and without the expense of paper, ink, and printer wear and tear. Of course, you can always print out all or part of your downloaded document(s) when needed.

8

Shortcuts and Gimmicks

THIS CHAPTER COVERS:

SHORT CUT

ECLIPSE

Computer-Assisted Instruction

Help

Request

THIS CHAPTER is full of automated shortcuts: ways to do things much more quickly, efficiently, and competently. You can get along without everything here (sort of the way you can get along without sliced bread—just get up early enough to mix and knead and bake and slice your own, and clean up), but you and your billfold will be glad you don't have to.

SHORT CUT

One of the most useful shortcuts on LEXIS is called *SHORT CUT*. The SHORT CUT feature allows you to save time by entering multiple commands together so that you bypass various menus and prompts. SHORT CUT lets you enter your client ID, library and file choices, search request, and cite format as a single entry. A SHORT CUT command looks like this:

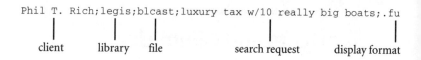

```
Phil T. Rich;legis;blcast;luxury tax w/10 really big boats;.fu
```
client   library   file   search request   display format

Each command is separated by a semicolon (no space is needed). You can use SHORT CUT whenever you need to enter several commands in succession. One of the most convenient tricks is to use ; ; after a file name to repeat a search. If, for example, you want to repeat a search that is several lines long in another library, there is no need to retype the entire search. Just type .cl;library;file;;display format (.cl;genfed;mega;;.ci.) and you are done. Besides saving the time and trouble of retyping, you avoid mistakes possible in reentering the search. Note: You must press Enter after typing in the search text in order to begin a search.

To use SHORTCUT to go straight to your search results when first signing on	Type your client ID; library; file; search request; display format.
To print a document without wading through the destination and confirmation screens	Type .pr;.fu;y;.nd. That command breaks down to .pr (for print); .fu (or other display format); y (for yes, yes, a thousand times yes, I really do want to print this); and .nd (for go on to the next document ASAP, I've got places to be, people to see, and a Ho-Ho in the vending machine with my name on it).
To repeat the same search in a different library	Type .cl (for change library); library; file;; (that's two semicolons in a row after the file name, to repeat the search you just ran); and a display format. (example—.cl;genfed;mega;;.kw)
To repeat the same search in a different file	Type .cf (change files), file name,;; (two semicolons after the file name),

	and a `display format.` (example–`.cf;courts;;.ci`)
Even just doing a new search is a little quicker with SHORT CUT (you save waiting for the query screen to materialize)	Type `.ns` (new search) `;search request.` (example–`.ns;covenant w/5 compet!`)
To enter a modification	Enter `m;` and `your modification.` (example–`m;and potatoes`)
Any two commands can be stacked, no matter how piddling (a technical term meaning trivial or itty-bitty)	example–`.np;.fu`
To enter a FOCUS request	Type `.fo;` followed by your focus request (example–`.fo;potatoes`)
To change to a new client ID and do a new search	Type `.c` (to change client ID), client name, `.ns` (new search), `search request, display format.` (example–`.c;A. Client;.ns;per-simmon w/9 lethal;.ci`)

SHORT CUT requires the barest minimum of forethought, which it rewards handsomely with time and money savings and freedom from the tedious chore of watching the same screens slowly scroll by time and time again (if you have a slow modem, you'll find using SHORT CUT especially sanity preserving). Another great feature of SHORT CUT is that it makes its user look extremely cool and competent. Be sure to use this whenever a senior partner walks by, as if to say, "Ah, yes, knowledgeable and invaluable to the organization as I am, I need not even wait for prompts. My commands go directly to the nerve center of LEXIS, bypassing the gauntlet of menu screens that daunt lesser mortals … good day, Sir or Madam!" A few cavalier keystrokes and the secrets of the universe are revealed to you. You are master of all you survey. If James Bond had access to LEXIS, he would definitely use SHORT CUT.

Some SHORT CUT searches are so cool you should really bring a date. Suppose you need to print up the text of a case and its Shepard's table. You type

```
LEXSEE 201 US 1;.pr;.fu;y;SHEP;.pr;y;.so.
```

If you can touch type, you can do this with barely a glance at the screen and voilà, you are off-line and your printer is scrambling to keep up with you before your awestruck audience can imagine what your genius has wrought. This will win you nearly as much awe from colleagues as being able to figure tips in your head.

Any LEXIS command can be used in a SHORT CUT request. A list of LEXIS commands are included here for your convenience:

CHANGE LIBRARY	.cl
CHANGE FILE	.cf
NEW SEARCH	.ns
CITE	.ci
FULL	.fu
KWIC	.kw
VARIABLE KWIC	.vk#
SEGMENTS	.se
FIRST PAGE	.fp
NEXT PAGE	.np
PREVIOUS PAGE	.pp
FIRST DOCUMENT	.fd
NEXT DOCUMENT	.nd
PREVIOUS DOCUMENT	.pd
DISPLAY DIFFERENT LEVEL	.dl#

FOCUS	.fo
EXIT FOCUS	.ef
MAIL IT	.mi
PRINT ALL	.pa
PRINT DOCUMENT	.pr
SHEPARD'S	SHEP
AUTO-CITE	AC
LEXCITE	LEXCITE
LEXSEE	LEXSEE
LEXSTAT	LEXSTAT
EXIT SERVICE	.es
RESUME	RESUME
MODIFY	M
KEEP	.KEEP
LOG	.LOG
SIGN OFF	.so

ECLIPSE

ECLIPSE automatically updates a search every month, week, or business day according to your specifications. It does this without any help from you; you don't even need to sign on during this time. The results can be sent to your stand-alone printer or stored so that they are available for you to peruse on-line at your convenience. ECLIPSE searches cost $12 per daily report, $16 per business-daily report, $18 per weekly report, and $24 per monthly report. ECLIPSE updates cost less than rerunning the same query as a regular search, so they are the way to go if you need to update the same search regularly.

How to Use ECLIPSE

To use ECLIPSE, you need to be looking at the results of the search you want to update. If you aren't there already, just run the search you wish to save (pick a library and file and run the search in the usual way). Once you have the results, type `sav` (for save). You will be prompted to name the search. You can use any name with up to 12 characters. Try to think of a name that will remind you of what the search is about to save time and confusion.

You will then be prompted to choose how often the search will be updated (every day, every business day, weekly, or monthly) and whether the results should be sent to your stand-alone printer or stored for you to look at on-line. Note that it costs more to have your search updated every day than it does to have it updated every business day and that there is no point in having it updated daily if you won't be looking at the results on the weekend. ECLIPSE updates are run in the morning of the days you specify.

■ Should you have your ECLIPSE results stored on-line or sent to a stand-alone printer? Ordinarily on-line storage is better, since it gives you a chance to read your results before you pay to print them. You have fewer piles of possibly irrelevant paper to deal with, correspondingly fewer dead trees on your conscience, and one less chance that something important will be lost or disposed of by someone in your office before you ever see it. ■

Finally, you will be prompted to specify the format for your results (CITE, KWIC, VAR-KWIC, or FULL: see Chapter 5) and to confirm (`y` for yes) that you want the search saved in ECLIPSE, to be updated automatically, or not (`n` for no). If you elected to have your ECLIPSE results sent to a printer instead of stored on-line, you can start the print-fest right away by entering `r` for a printed report showing the results of the search you just saved.

To return to the screen you were viewing before you went into ECLIPSE, type . es (for exit service). You need to do this even if you are going to begin a new ECLIPSE search next, since you have to get to the results of that new search before you can save it in ECLIPSE.

How to View ECLIPSE Results

If you elected to have your ECLIPSE results sent to your stand-alone printer, they will print automatically and be waiting for you in the printer tray or, if your stand-alone is as busy, surly, and poorly attended as most, all over the floor in front of the printer.

If you elected to have your ECLIPSE results stored on-line, there will be a message when you log on notifying you when you have new ECLIPSE results waiting. You can view those results by typing . ss for the Select Service menu and then typing rec (to recall a previously saved ECLIPSE search). You will see a list of ECLIPSE searches (if you have more than one) with the names of those searches with new results highlighted. Choose a search and type r (for retrieve) to see the results of that search.

How to Print or Store ECLIPSE Results

Once retrieved, ECLIPSE results can be printed and stored like any other search results. See Chapter 7.

Updating an ECLIPSE Search

LEXIS updates your ECLIPSE search automatically at the intervals you specify when you enter the search. If you want to update the search at some other time, type . ss (select service) to get the service menu. Type rec (recall a previously saved ECLIPSE search) and select the search you want to update from the list of searches given. If you have been having your ECLIPSE results sent to your stand-alone printer, a screen like Figure 8.1 will appear. You can retrieve all updating documents added since you first set up the

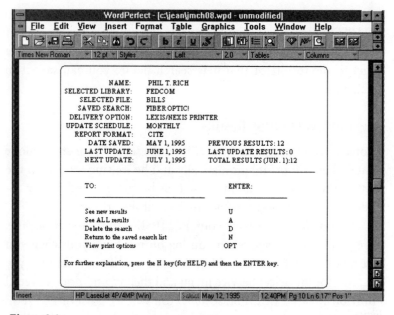

Figure 8.1

ECLIPSE search by typing a (for all), or only those documents added since the last automatic update by typing u (for update).

If you have been having your results stored to be viewed on-line, a screen like Figure 8.2 will appear. Your only choice in this case is to retrieve documents added since the last automatic update, by typing r (for retrieve).

If you are viewing other search results when you enter ECLIPSE, the computer will ask if you want to leave the old search results to run the ECLIPSE search or not. Choose yes or no; you know the drill by now.

If you want to change the intervals at which the search will be updated automatically, you can change your ECLIPSE request accordingly. If at this or any other point you decide you want out of ECLIPSE, type .es (for exit service).

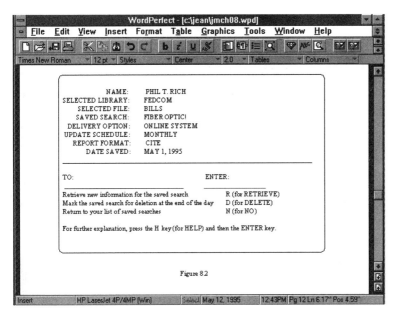

Figure 8.2

Figure 8.2

Changing an ECLIPSE Search

You can modify an ECLIPSE search to run in a different library and/or file, change the intervals at which it is to be updated, change the display format, or change the wording of the search itself. When you change an ECLIPSE search, all the results of the original search are discarded, so be sure to print or store them before you change the search if you want to hold on to them.

To change an ECLIPSE search, follow the steps for setting up a new ECLIPSE search and when, as the final step, you are prompted to enter a name for the search, use the same name as you used for the original you want to change. The computer will tell you that a search already exists with that name and ask you to confirm (y for yes) that you want to replace it. Why change an old search instead of just making a new one? Because you will still be paying for every update to the old one until it is replaced or deleted.

Deleting an ECLIPSE Search

To get rid of an ECLIPSE search, type `.ss` to pull up the select service menu, type `rec` (for recall a previously saved ECLIPSE search), and press Enter. A list of your ECLIPSE searches will be displayed and you will be prompted to select the one you wish to do in. Then a screen like Figure 8.1 or 8.2 will appear, depending upon whether you elected to have your ECLIPSE results sent to your stand-alone printer or stored on-line. Type `d` (for delete) and press Enter, and your ECLIPSE search is deleted. (It truly is no more. It has gone to swim with the fish in concrete sneakers.) If you have a change of heart after you delete but before midnight on the same day, you can bring the search back to life by typing `rec` at the Select Service menu and following the instructions on the screen for recalling a search. After midnight of the day they are deleted, old ECLIPSE searches move irrevocably onward to a better place and cannot be recalled.

Computer-Assisted Instruction

LEXIS provides a series of LEXIS "lessons" on-line, which it calls Computer-Assisted Instructions, or CAI. To access these lessons, sign on and type `.ss` to get to the Select Service menu. Choose CAI to access the lessons. The CAI database is free, including connect time.

Help

On-line help is available at any time by typing `h` and pressing Enter. The text you see is keyed to the screen you were looking at when you requested help, but you can move to help on other subjects by searching for a help topic, following the on-screen directions. If you are using Windows, the Help screens you see are inexplicably different depending on whether you get into help by typing h or by clicking on Help. The screens you get by typing h are more complete.

Request

You can get a report of where you are and what you have done since you signed on for the current research session by entering r. You might want to print request screens, such as the one in Figure 8.3, for your records. (More accurately, you might not *want* to, but it is probably a good idea. If nothing else you can show it to the judge during the hearing to determine whether your fees were ludicrously overinflated.)

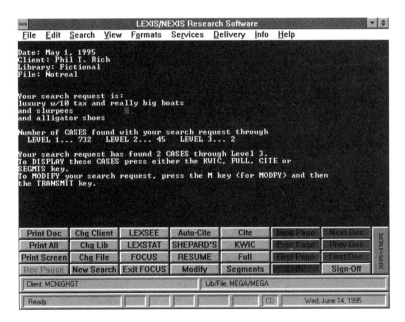

Figure 8.3

CHAPTER 8.   QUICK REFERENCE PAGE

Request = `r`

To save a search to be run in ECLIPSE = `sav`

To view ECLIPSE results on-line or access Computer-Assisted Instruction, use the Select Service menu = `.ss`

To exit ECLIPSE = `.es`

To get help = `h`

9

Using LEXIS to Find a Job

THIS CHAPTER COVERS:

Job-hunting files

Employer Directory

Martindale-Hubbell®

Judicial Clerkship Directory

Public Interest Employer Directory

Congressional Member Profile Report

United States Government Manual

Federal Careers for Attorneys

Law-Related Careers in the Federal Government

Directory of Bankruptcy Attorneys

Job-Hunting Files

The following files contain useful information for job hunters. They primarily identify marks (er, "employers") to beg (er, "apply") for a job. They can be searched the way other LEXIS files can, using terms and connectors, Freestyle, segment searches, and so on (see Chapters 2 and 3). All of these files are in the CAREER library except for Martindale-Hubbell, which has a library all to itself (MARHUB).

Employer Directory (CAREER Library, EMPDIR File)

This is a directory of employers who anticipate openings for law students, including first- and second-year summer jobs. Firms provide a law firm profile and description of potential positions. The file is updated three times a year, so it pays to look again now and then. More than 1,200 employers, most (but not all) of whom are large firms from large cities, are profiled as of this writing. Documents (profiles) retrieved display in alphabetical order by state name, followed by city name and firm name. The following segments are available in the EMPDIR file:

SEGMENT	EXPLANATION
address	Employer's address, phone and fax numbers (where available)
assoc	All associate segments
afro-am-assoc	Number of African American associates
asian-am-assoc	Number of Asian associates
disabled-assoc	Number of disabled associates
gay-assoc	Number of openly gay associates
hispanic-assoc	Number of Hispanic associates
men-assoc	Number of male associates
native-assoc	Number of Native American associates
women-assoc	Number of female associates
benefits	Sick leave, profit sharing, parental leave, etc. Note that insurance has its own segment.
city-state	The city and state where the employer is located.
current-staff	How many of the current staff are partners, of counsel, senior attorneys, associates, paralegals, and support staff.
firm-composition	For each of the last three years, lists how many partners, associates, senior associates, summer associates, men, women, African Americans, Asian Americans, Hispanics, Native Americans,

SEGMENT	EXPLANATION
	gay attorneys, and disabled attorneys were employed.
hiring-attorney	Name and phone of hiring attorney
insurance	Do employees get insurance? life? health? disability? dental?
interviews	Dates when employer will be interviewing at specific schools
name	Name of employer (firm, organization, or agency)
new-assoc	What new associates can expect—beginning salaries, work schedules, unlimited coffee and yellow pads, help with moving expenses or not.
openings	Number of current openings and the number of people employed during the last three years.
other-offices	Locations of employer's offices other than the one at the main address given. Each office has its own profile in a separate document.
partners	Number of partners who are male, female, African-American, Asian-American, disabled, gay, Native-American, or Hispanic.
partnership	Employer's promotion statistics.
part-time-work	Does the employer allow part-time work, or is the very idea that an employee might have any life outside of the office intolerable to them?
practice-area	How many staff work in each of the firm's practice areas (i.e., tax).
pro-bono policy	Employer's pro bono policy (i.e., do they encourage or forbid it?)
promo-consider	Number of years before employer will even *consider* making you a partner.
1L-resume-dates	Cutoff dates for first-year student résumé submissions.

(continued)

SEGMENT	EXPLANATION
staff-turnover	Do people flee the firm as soon as they can, or do they stay forever?
summer-assoc	What summer associates can expect—salary, work schedule, whether they are required to stand and salute each time a senior partner goes by.
travel	Whether employer pays all or part of travel expenses for interviewees.

Retrieving Employer Profiles in EMPDIR

TO FIND	SEARCH FOR
firms in a given location	City-state(city name and/or state name). Example: `city-state(Dover Delaware)`.
firms that practice a given specialty	Practice-area(description of specialty). Note that there is no standard terminology employed for specialties—employers describe their practices with the one- or two-word descriptions of their choice. This makes it a good idea to search for as many synonyms as you can think of. Example: `practice-area(family or domestic)`.
a specific firm	Name(firm's name, with connectors or universal characters if you aren't positive about it). Example: you want to find the profile for the firm Big and Bucks (or maybe it was Biggs or Bigg, and maybe they have another partner now). Use `name(big! w/3 bucks)`.
a firm in a given location with a given specialty	City-state (——) and practice-area (——). Example: `city-state(sarasota) and practice-area(tax)`.

Printing a Mailing List from EMPDIR

You can print a mailing list of addresses of prospective employers you find by typing `address, p`. You will be prompted to select the addresses you want by document number (you need to keep track of these as you go along) or type `many` to get the addresses of all the employers retrieved by your current search. Confirm your document delivery and destination as usual (see Chapter 6). You can then use your mailing list to print envelopes or address labels and be on your way to the land of the gainfully employed with plenty of time left over for whatever it is you are doing now.

Martindale-Hubbell (MARHUB Library)

Martindale-Hubbell is the largest directory of attorneys and law firms in America. It consists of files of practice profiles for individual attorneys and firms. United States attorneys and firms are listed in the USPROF file, Canadian attorneys and firms are listed in the CPROF file, and attorneys and firms outside Canada or the United States and its territories are listed in the IPROF file. All three of these files are combined in the ALLDIR file. Patent and trademark practices can be searched separately in USPAT, CPAT, and IPAT (for the U.S., Canadian and international firms, respectively).

There is a file listing legal services and suppliers (USSERV); files listing the locations of U.S., Canadian, and international colleges, universities, and law schools (USLIST, CLIST, and ILIST); and a file listing U.S. government lawyers (USGOVT). Firms can pay to have their firm's profile (which they supply) included in the USBIO or CBIO file (USBIO has U.S. firms, CBIO has Canadian ones). Corporations can do the same in the USCORP file.

■ All of the separate Martindale-Hubbell files mentioned here can be combined into ALLDIR to be searched simultaneously. ■

The contents of the MARHUB library correspond to the contents of the print version of the Martindale-Hubbell directory and are updated when the publisher supplies updates to LEXIS. Law firms have their own profile documents in addition to separate profile documents for each attorney in the firm. Attorney profiles contain detailed biographical information and some information about their firms. Firm profiles have more detailed information about firms than the attorney profiles do.

The following segments are available in MARHUB profiles:

SEGMENT	EXPLANATION
section	Section of Martindale-Hubbell books. For example: Practice Profiles Section.
name	Name of lawyer or firm.
location	Name of law practice.
born	When and where lawyer was born. (Firms are not born. Hatched?)
admitted	When and where lawyer was admitted to practice.
college	Where lawyer got undergraduate degree.
law school	Where lawyer got J.D.
text	Lawyer's work experience.
practice	Type of practice.
branches	Where firm has branch offices.
languages	Languages (besides English and Legalese) spoken by lawyer or at least one of the lawyers in firm.
firm-profile	When firm was established; things they brag about.
firm	The firm a lawyer is a member of. (Used in profiles of lawyers. Firm name is under "name" in firm profiles.)
clients	Clients that the firm or lawyer has and believes you will be impressed by.
position	Lawyer's title—associate, junior coffee-fetcher, etc.

SEGMENT	EXPLANATION
concentration	What the firm or lawyer spends most time on, or wishes they spent most time on, i.e. glam. law (glamorous and dramatic litigation, such as that featured on *L.A. Law*), legal services for the obscenely rich.
city	City where firm or attorney practices.
state	State where firm or attorney practices.
location	Address, county, phone and fax numbers of firm or attorney.
reported cases	Citations to reported cases in which attorney was involved.
personnel	Names of personnel employed by firm (may include some non-attorneys).
special agencies	Agencies attorney is involved with.
service	Whether attorney served in armed forces (and which branch).
corp-profile	Profile of corporation for in-house counsel.
school	The name of a school in the colleges, universities, and law schools listing. (Note that there is no school field in the practice profiles. To find the law school a lawyer attended, search the law school field. To find the undergraduate institution he or she attended, search the college field.)
services	The service(s) provided by an organization listed in the services and suppliers directory (the SERVE file, a part of the ALLDIR group file).
firm-size or dept-size	Available in the paid biographies, these fields can be searched but are not displayed on-screen like other fields. You can search for a firm or department of a certain size (firm = 10) or one larger or smaller than a specified number of members (firm > 5).

Sample Martindale-Hubbell Searches

TO FIND	SEARCH FOR
alums of your college with a given specialty	`college(clemson) and concentration(tax)`
firms with more than 25 attorneys in Boston	`firm-size(>25) and city(boston)`
Mickey Dolan's lawyer	`client(mickey w/2 dolan)`
your old law-school roommate	`name(al w/3 brown) and law school(Whatsamata U.)`

Printing a Mailing List from Martindale-Hubbell

You can't. At least not directly. First, there is no address field, and the location field has no name in it. You can print the citations for the firms you retrieve to get the names and addresses, but you'll also have some other garbage you'll have to clean up by hand. The big danger in making a mailing list from Martindale-Hubbell is that you'll send 72 copies of your résumé to the same firm because you weren't paying attention to which profiles are law-firm profiles and which are lawyer profiles, possibly of lawyers in a firm you've already selected for your mailing list. Avoid this by searching only for firms: adding AND not born will do the trick. Even so, you should proof your list carefully to avoid making a big, not-so-hot impression on your intended employer to be.

Judicial Clerkship Directory (CAREER Library, JCLERK File)

The JCLERK file contains application information for clerkships with federal judges and magistrates and the judges of the highest court of each state. Each document lists information about a judge or magistrate and the clerks they have hired in the past, along with their preferences and openings for current clerks. A mailing list of judges can be generated by typing `address, p` once you have retrieved your results. Be sure your letter is addressed to the contact listed rather than to the judge herself; they give these contacts for a reason and are unlikely to be impressed that you don't bother to use them.

Public Interest Employer Directory (CAREER Library, PUBINT File)

The PUBINT file contains employers who plan to hire law students for summer or permanent positions in the coming year. When you use PUBINT, information and instructions for searching the file and generating a mailing list display automatically (and since law students don't pay for on-line time, I won't repeat them here).

Congressional Member Profile Report (CAREER, LEGIS, or GENFED Libraries; MEMBR File)

The MEMBR files of these libraries contain official biographical information about members of Congress. The following segments are included:

SEGMENT	EXPLANATION
name	Member's name.
address	Member's Washington office address.
election-status	Incumbent or not.
election year	Year member is up for reelection.
party	Political party.
office	Title—Senior Senator of Maine, for example.
region	Region of U.S. the member represents.

(*continued*)

SEGMENT	EXPLANATION
sworn-in date	
term	What number term they are in (example: 3rd).
sex	
religion	
race	
spouse	Spouse's name is given, presumably so researchers can decide whether it would be prudent to try to fix up member with first cousin from Winnipeg (or maybe so lobbyists can address holiday cards properly).
occupation	Member's day job.
education	What, where, and when.
military service	What and when.
biography	Birth, high school, and everything else member is proud of.
assignments	Committees member is assigned to.
leadership-caucus	Leadership positions and caucus memberships.
staff	Washington and home office addresses and phone numbers.

United States Government Manual
(CAREER Library, USGM File)

This file contains the complete text of the United States Government ment Manual, which lists addresses, phone numbers, and identifying information on government agencies. Each agency description lists primary officials, a brief history of the agency and statement of its purpose, the legislative authority for its existence, a description of what it does, and a plethora of contact information. You can generate a mailing list from your search results by typing `address, p.`

The following segments are included in the USGM:

SEGMENT	EXPLANATION
agency	Name of the agency.
address	Address and phone number of the agency.
sources	Who to call or write for more information on specific subjects.
contact	Who to call or write for more information about the agency in general.

Federal Careers for Attorneys (CAREER Library, FCA File)

Descriptions of the legal work and application requirements of federal legal offices. Each document lists an agency, which governmental branch they are part of, a description of the job, and application information.

Law-Related Careers in the Federal Government (CAREER Library, LRCFG File)

The LRCFG file provides information on (yes, you guessed it!) law-related careers in the federal government. Here's what you get: job descriptions, number of positions, number of men and women holding these positions, grade levels, average salaries, number of overseas jobs, and application information.

Directory of Bankruptcy Attorneys
(CAREER or BKRTCY Library, BKDIR File)

This file contains the full text of the Directory of Bankruptcy Attorneys published by Prentice-Hall Law and Business: more than you could ever want to know about bankruptcy attorneys unless (heaven forbid) you want to hire one or be one. It includes profiles of bankruptcy lawyers, law firms, and courts.

10

NEXIS, MEDIS, and Other Not-for-Lawyers-Only Services

IN THIS CHAPTER, WE COVER
THE FOLLOWING SERVICES:

NEXIS

MEDIS

Associated Press Political Service (APOLIT)

The National Automated Accounting Research System
  (NAARS) Service

Financial Information Service

Country Information Service

Public Records Online Service

M EAD DATA CENTRAL had already made a great deal of
money on its LEXIS service when it came up with the
idea of adding NEXIS (apparently meaning, at least secondarily,
"not-so-LEXIS"); MEDIS; and other services designed to expand its
market to non-lawyers. All of these services appear on the
LEXIS/NEXIS menu when you sign on.

NEXIS

NEXIS contains a dizzying array of full-text non-legal information
from newspapers, magazines, journals, wire services, newsletters,
and other sources. Lawyers find all this information invaluable in the

fact-finding stage of their research (and in wasting time looking up trivia while they should be working). There is more information on more topics than you could process in a lifetime, and it is all available at the touch of a button (well, OK, several buttons and a wallet). NEXIS is sort of like Nintendo for the information junkie. Once hooked, you'll wonder how you ever got along without it.

The time-wasting possibilities of NEXIS are endless (you'll never have to resort to trimming your nails to procrastinate again), but the legitimate legal practice uses are pretty remarkable too. You can find newspaper articles about cases settled out of court, information about the manufacturers of a product that injured your client, design and performance standards for the product, the names of people who hold patents on similar devices, the financial situations of companies, and so on. The list goes on and on. If you're looking for an expert witness, you can search scientific and technical journals and conference reports to find someone who has written an article or given a speech on the topic in question. Or you can use the EXPERT file in the LEXREF library, which contains information on more than 5,000 technical or medical experts. Did I say the possibilities are nearly endless? Well, it was true that time too.

OK, so I've convinced you that NEXIS is really great (or maybe I haven't, but you're still reading anyway). So how do you use it? Good news at last! It is very, *very* much like LEXIS. NEXIS libraries come up on the LEXIS menu screen (under the NEXIS heading). They are made up of files that you search pretty much like other files. Of course, the files have different information and different segments (enter `.se` to see the segments available in a file you are currently in), but you can make the leap pretty easily.

■ Some NEXIS documents have a Graphic segment, but no graphics are available on NEXIS, so what you get is a line telling you what the graphic in the printed version shows. Then if you really want the graphic, you have to track down the printed version. ■

Descriptions of the NEXIS files and their contents are available in the *NEXIS Product Guide*. You can look up specific publications to see if they are included in any of the NEXIS files using the *NEXIS and Related Services Alphabetical List*. Descriptions of each file are also available on-line through the GUIDE file. To see a list of segments available in the file you are in, type `.se`.

Most files in NEXIS are full-text, but some have only abstracts. These are kindly labeled ABS and are grouped together in the ALL-ABS file.

■ NEXIS can earn its keep by telling you what you need to know about people, products, lawsuits, companies, and so on. Has Mr. Q been sued before? Has he testified before in a manner you might be able to use to impeach him? Has he been written up in the papers for doing noteworthy things?

Are there other lawsuits pending that are similar to the one you are working on? Have a lot of people been involved in similar accidents with three-wheel vehicles? Is a merger in the works for your client's nemesis? If it has been written up in major papers, magazines, or other sources, you can now get your hands on it. ■

NEXIS Libraries

LIBRARY NAME	LIBRARY CONTENTS
BACKGR	◆ News Background Information
	Apparently Mead considers news background information to be information on earthquakes, floods, hurricanes, hazardous wastes, serial killers, mass murderers, AIDS, plane crashes, Lyme disease, and abortion. If it doesn't make you wring your hands, it's not in here.
BANKS	◆ Banking News and Information
	BANKS includes Investext Industry Reports on more than 65 worldwide investment banks, Predicasts banking information, assorted newsletters, etc.

(continued)

LIBRARY NAME	LIBRARY CONTENTS
BUSFIN	◆ Business and Finance News and Information Business, investment, and merger acquisitions news.
BUSREF	◆ Business Reference Information BUSREF includes company directories, reference publications, information on business opportunities, and biographical information on politicians and other famous people.
CMPCOM	◆ Computers and Communications News and Information CMPCOM has news sources and company/industry reports relevant to computers, electronics, and communications.
CMPGN	◆ Campaign News and Information CMPGN covers election issues, candidate biographies, political contributions, and voting records of members of Congress.
ENTERT	◆ Entertainment News and Information ENTERT has the latest news, awards, finances, company/industry reports, reviews, biographies, etc.
EXEC	◆ Executive Branch News and Information EXEC features news coverage of the executive branch and federal government agencies and also includes regulatory information, the full text of public laws, and proposed state regulations.
LEGIS	◆ Legislation Full-text bills, bill tracking and predictions of the likelihood of success for various bills, the full text of *Congressional Record*, U.S. public laws, state advance legislative services.
LEGNEW	◆ Legal News and Information LEGNEW contains news about the legal profession, including law-firm management literature, verdicts and settlements, bar journals, and legal newspapers and newsletters.

LIBRARY NAME	LIBRARY CONTENTS

LEXPAT ◆ U.S. Patent and Trademark Office Information

LEXPAT contains the full text of utility patents since 1975 and plant and design patents since December 1976. The CLASS file has patent numbers for all patents since 1790 by class, and the CLMNL file is the *U.S. Patent and Trademark Office Manual of Classification.* The *Index to U.S. Patent Classification* is in the INDEX file.

MARKET ◆ Markets and Industries News and Information

MARKET collects sources covering advertising, marketing, public relations, sales, demographics, product announcements and reviews, industry overviews, etc.

NEWS ◆ General News and Information

NEWS is the largest NEXIS library, with the full text of more than 2,300 news sources (including newspapers, magazines, journals, newsletters, wire services, and broadcast transcripts) and abstracts from over 1,000 more. It is probably the most useful source of general information.

PEOPLE ◆ Biographical Information

What famous people had for breakfast and think about tort reform or astrologers.

SPORTS ◆ Sports News

SPORTS is composed of the full text of *Sports Illustrated* and the *Sporting News* plus the sports sections of major newspapers and newswires.

TOPNWS ◆ Top News

TOPNWS offers current (choose today's or the last two weeks') top news stories from around the world (updated every 60 minutes; transcripts added within three hours of broadcast).

Special NEXIS Search Considerations

Although you search NEXIS files the same way you search LEXIS files, the sheer volume of information available in NEXIS means that more accuracy is often needed to avoid retrieving a totally unmanageable number of documents. Segment searching is always a good way to make searches more accurate, whether you are working in NEXIS or LEXIS (see Chapter 3). Headline is an especially useful NEXIS segment, since it allows you to search for articles in which your subject is a primary topic rather than a brief or incidental mention. A date restriction usually thins the ranks of results admirably (see Chapter 3). Another good desperation tactic is to search for multiple mentions of your topic in the same document ("cats W/100 cats W/100 cats"), on the reasonable assumption that articles that mention a topic repeatedly have more to say about it.

MEDIS

The MEDIS service contains medical information. This information is of obvious interest to physicians and the lawyers who sue or defend them. It is composed of two libraries, MEDLINE and GENMED.

LIBRARY NAME	LIBRARY CONTENTS
MEDLINE	This library contains abstracts (not full text) from more than 3,500 medical journals since 1966. The abstracts are prepared by the authors. Once you have located an abstract of an article of potential interest, you will have to resort to ordering the full text from the publisher or visiting a medical library. You may be able to obtain the articles free of charge through interlibrary loan through your public library or some other library with which you are affiliated.
GENMED	This library is a collection of full-text materials from a more limited array of medical journals. Coverage dates vary from journal to journal.

Associated Press Political Service (APOLIT)

APOLIT contains election-related information: polls, congressional ratings, an election calendar, candidate biographies, and campaign news.

The National Automated Accounting Research System (NAARS) Service

NAARS contains the full text of audited annual reports from companies traded on the New York or American Stock Exchanges, ranked by *Fortune*, or put on margin by the Federal Reserve. It also has an accounting literature file.

Financial Information Service

LIBRARY NAME	LIBRARY CONTENTS
INVEST ◆	Analysts Research Library
	Company and industry reports by Investext®. This library has menu-driven searching unlike other LEXIS/NEXIS libraries. Instructions appear on the screen when you select this library.
COMPNY ◆	Company Library
	Company profiles and abstracts of filings for more than 11,000 public companies, industry research reports, and much, much more.
QUOTE ◆	Quote Library
	This library finds real-time equity quotes and market information plus historical quotes. A unique service in QUOTE allows you to save a quote or search for one from any point in your research by typing . qt and following directions on the screen.

Country Information Service

This service provides information on conditions and events that affect the practice of business or law in various countries and areas. The following libraries are available:

LIBRARY NAME	LIBRARY CONTENTS
ASIAPC	Asia and Pacific Rim News and Information
CANADA	Canadian News and Information
EUROPE	European News and Information
MDEAFR	Middle Eastern and African News and Information
NSAMER	North and South American News and Information
WORLD	World News and Information (combination of above)

Individual files within these libraries deal with specific topics or countries.

Public Records Online Service

This service consists of five libraries of public records information:

LIBRARY NAME	LIBRARY CONTENTS
LIENS	Personal Property Liens—from CA, IL, MA, MD, NY, PA, and TX
INCORP®	Corporation and Partnership Records (limited to 17 states)
DOCKET	Court Dockets—for CA, NY, and PA
ASSETS	Tax assessor and deed transfer records for counties and major metropolitan areas in 34 states.
VERDCT	Extensive verdict and settlement information in civil cases, with case summaries.

LIBRARY NAME	LIBRARY CONTENTS
FINDER	Person and Business Locator Information—a nation-wide directory of more than 111 million people listed in phone books and public records. Individual state files help narrow down possibilities if you're looking for a John Smith.

You can place an order for copies of public records on-line by entering LEXDOC. Instructions and choices are listed on the screen. LEXIS Document Services provides filing and searching assistance with public records, with special services available on request. Call 800-634-9738 for more information.

11

CheckCite

What Is CheckCite?

CheckCite is a program that finds citations in a document and checks them on-line automatically. It gives you a report of Auto-Cite and Shepard's results. It also retrieves the full text of cases for you using LEXSEE. CheckCite can work from a list of citations or from word-processed text containing citations, such as a brief. It can be customized to retrieve only the information you want. You pay the same rate per citation as if you had searched manually, but you save preparation and on-line time. CheckCite is available from the Jurisoft Division of Mead Data Central at 1-800-543-6862.

CheckCite comes with its own 164-page manual, which is very thorough but has no index. In the interest of saving you some time and irritation, I have condensed the basic indispensable information here. Consult your manual if you need additional help.

■ **EMERGENCY APPLICATION OF THIS CHAPTER**
If your CheckCite program is already installed and you need to get through this faster than humanly possible so that you can get to the courthouse and defend a wrongly condemned widow and her seven doe-eyed children, then by all means skip to the section on basic cite checking with default options and see if you can't wing it from there. If you get a lot of unintelligible error messages or want to do more complicated things, you will have to read further—but otherwise you may make out all right. After all, you are a bright and enterprising sort, as demonstrated by the fact that you have elected to consult this fine publication. ■

Hardware and Software Requirements

To use CheckCite, you must have

1. A LEXIS account and ID.

2. An IBM-compatible computer with
   ◆ 280K of free memory (more is much better)
   ◆ 1.5 MB of free space on your hard disk (more is better)
   ◆ MS-DOS 2.0 or higher (newer)

3. A modem that works with your LEXIS software

If all this sounds like a foreign language, don't panic. There is an 800 number (1-800-543-6862) staffed by knowledgeable people who are determined to help you and who have been specifically forbidden to call you names or laugh out loud at your pitiful lack of computer savvy.

Installation

1. Do whatever you have to do to get your computer to offer you a DOS prompt (this looks like C>).

2. Put CheckCite disk 1 in a disk drive (let's say drive A).

3. Type A: and press Enter.

4. Type INSTALL and press Enter.

5. Follow the on-screen prompts until the system tells you installation is complete. It lies. There is more.

6. Type CHECKCITE and press Enter. If you have been living right, the Main menu will appear on the screen.

7. Select the SEARCH category from the menu by typing S and pressing Enter. Use the Down key to highlight the Citation Form option and type A if your cites are in Harvard *Bluebook* form or B if they are in California form. Press Esc.

8. Move the cursor back to the top of the screen using the Up Arrow key and type P. Then use the Down Arrow to highlight the Word Processor option, select the letter that corresponds to your word processor, and press the Esc key. If your word processor isn't listed, all is not lost: see "Defining a New Wordprocessor (ASDEF)" in your *CheckCite Manual.*

9. Go back to the top of the screen again and type A for Activity. Highlight Action to Perform and select C, Set Up CheckCite for Communication.

10. Type G to run the setup program. If prompted, type Y to record your changes.

11. Select Primary Connection Options. Choose the appropriate settings, and press Esc to return to the Setup menu.

■ To fill in all the information on the Primary Connection Options screen, you need to know how your communications equipment is set up. Even if your computer had fallen from the sky with communications ability fully in place, you would need some help at this point. If the person who is rumored in your office to be computer-competent has not fled the country to avoid all the people begging for help, try to get him or her to help you. Failing this, you may be able to figure things out by consulting your computer, network, or modem manuals. Finally, if all else fails, cross your fingers and try the following settings:

Connection Method:	Modem, unless you are using a network. If you are on a network, there is almost certainly a network administrator who can help you but is scurrying for cover at this very moment. Hunt this person down.
Serial Port:	Try Com1. If that doesn't work, try Com2.
Modem:	Select your model. If it isn't listed, check your modem manual to see if it is compatible with one of the models that is listed.
Parity:	Even.
Dial Method:	Tone or pulse, whichever your phones are.
Dial Mode:	Automatic.
Network Log-On Mode	Automatic.
Dialing Prefix:	The prefix you have to use when you dial out to order a pizza (in a lot of offices you have to dial 9, for example). Type in

	the prefix followed immediately by a comma, to tell the modem to pause the way you do when you dial.
Phone Number:	The number of your telecommunications network. If you don't know this number, have a look at the network directory supplied with your LEXIS software or call 1-800-543-6862.
Speed:	The speed of your modem: 300, 1200, 2400, 4800, 9600, or 14,400 baud. Check your modem manual. If you really have no idea, try guessing (older modems usually have slower baud rates, i.e., lower numbers).
Node Address (NUA):	If in doubt, try skipping this one. It may be entered automatically. This whole field disappears if you use Meadnet. ■

12. Optional Step. Select the first and/or second alternate connection options for the computer to try automatically if your first option fails. Return to the Setup menu.

13. Optional Step. If you are not sharing your CheckCite program with someone who uses a different LEXIS ID, select User Options and enter your LEXIS ID number so you don't have to enter it manually each time you use CheckCite. Press Esc to return to the Setup Menu.

14. Choose the Save and Exit Setup option. Select Y to save the configuration changes you've so laboriously selected, or press Esc to return to the Setup menu and have another go at it.

15. Rejoice. You have now installed CheckCite. There are lots of options you will need to fiddle with later, but you are ready to check the cites in a document now.

■ If you have trouble at any stage of the installation process, help is close at hand in several formats:

- ◆ Press F1 for on-screen help, which may or may not address your particular crisis.
- ◆ 1-800-543-6862 for real people who know how to make computers do what they want, and hopefully what you want.
- ◆ The CheckCite Manual. It is 164 pages long and has a forbidding black cover, but it is really very good.
- ◆ Your DOS manual.
- ◆ Your school-age son or daughter. Let's face it, they are just better at this stuff than we are. If you don't have an appropriately aged child, you may be able to borrow one. Many people are all too happy to loan them out. ■

Startup

Once you have installed and set up the program, you can start it up by typing `checkcite` at the DOS prompt. If the computer looks at you condescendingly and says, "bad command or file name," be sure you are in the right drive and directory (the one that contains the CheckCite program; consult your DOS manual if you are confused). You should see the Main menu.

■ SOME WARNINGS

If you use the name of an existing analysis report, the new one will replace the old one, not just peacefully coexist with it.

If the screen reads, "recover interrupted session" or "review last report," consult your manual. ■

The terms across the top of the Main menu screen (activity, document, etc.) are categories of options. Choose one by highlighting it with the Arrow keys and pressing Enter. Then use the Arrow keys to highlight the setting you want to change. Use the Left and

Right Arrow keys to see what options are available and select your choice by pressing Enter when you come to it. Press Esc to escape from a category when you are done with it.

The options available in each category are

◆ Activity: to check cites, select cite checking mode, reoutput last report, set up communications, modify dictionary, or choose an option sheet.

◆ Document: to identify the file you are checking, the file where the Analysis Report should go, and the client name.

■ A few hints about the document category: the "working document" refers to the document containing the cites you want to check. If you aren't sure what the name of the document you want to check is, type DIR and press Enter. Select the file name that sounds lucky by highlighting it and pressing Enter. To check a different directory, select (prev) <DIR> from the list. Select the directory you want from the displayed list and press Enter to see a list of the files in that directory.

Enter the name of the file you want the Analysis Report to be in unless you'd rather just read the report off the screen. If you are utterly devoid of creative impulses, press the Control key and B simultaneously, and the file will be named some suitably pedestrian but functional name for you. ■

◆ Search: to choose to search for *Bluebook-* or California-form cites.

◆ Report: to choose full-text (at $4.00 a cite), Auto-Cite (at $2.75 per cite), and/or Shepard's Service (at $2.75 per cite). If you don't want any one of these, make sure its option is set to NO.

◆ Preferences: to identify your word processor, what colors you like on the screen (no kidding), what kind of report you want, and whether you like cites underlined or italicized.

◆ Billing: to identify CheckCite use for a client (independent of LEXIS use, for which you will still be well and heartily billed). This allows you to bill clients for CheckCite-based overhead as you see fit.

◆ Go: after you have chosen from the other categories, use Go to start checking a document or modify the dictionary. If you are asked if you want to save your changes, enter Y if you do. If you choose N, all those selections you just made are vaporized instantaneously.

After you have chosen all your settings, you can tell the program to begin checking the document you specified by selecting Create an Analysis Report from the Go category. The screen will periodically offer an update on how things are going so you'll know progress is being made and will have something to look at while you wait.

When CheckCite is done, it will display an Analysis Report on the screen or send it to a file if you specified one. You can send a report from the screen to a file or print it using the menu on the Citation Display screen. You can read, print, or edit a file using your word processor.

Startup Shortcut

To save the time and trouble of starting CheckCite via the menu screens, you can run CheckCite under its default settings by entering a single line of commands. To use this direct method, type the following, separated by spaces, at the DOS prompt:

◆ `checkcite`

◆ The name of the document you want to check

◆ The name of your analysis file for this report (the file where the report will be sent). You can leave this out if you'd rather just read the Analysis Report on the screen.

♦ Two dollar signs. (You may put a client name between the dollar signs for billing purposes, or leave it out. The name will appear on your report and on your LEXIS bill.)

For example, if the name of the document you want to check for Joe Client is `your.doc` and your analysis file is `analysis.rep`, you would enter

```
CHECKCITE YOUR.DOC ANALYSIS.REP $JOE CLIENT$
```

and the computer will begin checking your document for cites.

Creating New Option Files

You can create option files (containing the particular CheckCite settings you have selected) and store them to be used with the direct method (startup shortcut) in place of the standard option file. This saves you the trouble of repeated voyages through the land of endless menu screens. You can create as many option files as you want and name them any name that has up to eight characters and an extension of up to three characters. To create such a file, type the following at the DOS prompt:

```
CHECKCITE/ MAKE NAME.OPT [+ your user ID if it is not
                          already programmed in]
```

and press Enter. The CheckCite menu will be displayed. Select the settings you want, press Esc and `Y` to save. You can now use this option file instead of the standard options by adding it, after a slash, to the direct method command:

```
CHECKCITE YOUR.DOC ANALYSIS.REP $JOE
         CLIENT$/OPTION.DOC
```

or you can make it the default option file (replacing the standard option file) by typing:

```
CHECKCITE/USE <OPTION.DOC> [+ID if necessary]
```

and pressing Enter.

Understanding a CheckCite Analysis Report

When CheckCite is done checking cites in the document you specified, it displays a summary document. If all is well, the summary will say "done" beside each service requested and "not requested" beside those, well, not requested.

If all is not well, you'll see one of the following messages:

MESSAGE	MEANING
Failed	Either the cite has a mistakenly (impossibly) high volume or page number or there is a communications error. Go back and check your communications settings if you haven't succeeded in checking other cites either.
Impossible	Citation is not available in service requested and/or cannot be checked by the service. It may be from an unpublished reporter or a reporter not covered by the service.
Requested	Cite has not been checked yet.
Cite may be wrong	Auto-Cite could not verify its existence. Check your cite.
Cite may be bad law	See Auto-Cite report.
Cite has negative treatment	See Shepard's report.
LEXIS equipment failure (try again later)	There is a problem with LEXIS's equipment, not yours.
Program failed earlier	Program stopped before this cite. Read back in the report to see where the problem was and try to fix it and start again.

MESSAGE	MEANING
Program halted on this citation	This is where the problem occurred.
Short form citation	Short-form cites can't be Shepardized.
Unexpected screen returned	Cite could not be checked because unexpected on-line information was coming in while the check was running. Try it again.
Unusable reporter(s)	Either your cite is missing a volume or page number, or the reporter in your cite needs to be added to the dictionary.
Wrong cite returned	Your cite was mysteriously transmuted into an alien cite en route. Try again.

If your cite appears to be non-existent, check your source again to see if you copied it wrong. If you don't still have the source, one option is to look the case name up in an appropriate digest table of cases. Another is to search an appropriate database for the case name. If you think your mistake is in a page number and you have the reporter volume, you can check the list of cases in the front of the volume to find the correct page.

The Auto-Cite Report

Auto-Cite generates a report for each cite you check, including short forms if they are in correct form and the long form appears earlier in the document. If your short form doesn't contain an "at," CheckCite assumes it is an erroneous long-form cite.

Once Auto-Cite has checked a cite in your document, it refers you back to that report for all subsequent appearances of the cite. You'll see a message like, "other Auto-Cite information located with citation #12." Information provided in an Auto-Cite report is the same as that provided on the screen when you use Auto-Cite manually (see Chapter 5).

The Shepard's Report

Shepard's presents a report similar to the Auto-Cite report for each cite it checks. CheckCite does *not* Shepardize short cites, but that shouldn't be a problem since you have presumably included the long form, as that will already have been checked. Information provided in a Shepard's report is the same as that provided on the screen when you use Shepard's manually (see Chapter 5).

The Full-Text Report

If you asked for the full text of cited cases, they will be included in the full-text report. One advantage of using CheckCite to retrieve the full text of cases is that it edits out the running headers from the top of each screen, underlines case titles cited in the text, and indents quoted paragraphs. This saves you some trouble if you need a presentable copy to work with. It also highlights footnotes, though I'm not sure how this is helpful.

Modifying the Dictionaries

CheckCite contains two dictionaries that enable it to identify cases, statutes, services, law reviews, court names, and history phrases. Note that although CheckCite only checks case citations, it has other types of citations in its dictionaries so that it will "know" not to display them on the Questionable Reporters screen of your Analysis Report, wasting time and space. One CheckCite dictionary is for California citation form (CALDFILE), and the other is for *Bluebook* form (DICTFILE). You can modify either dictionary to include particular citations or history phrases that a dictionary does not recognize or abbreviations or popular names of your choosing. You can also add terms that the computer mistakes for cites to the dictionaries' non-citation material list to keep them from reappearing on your Analysis Reports as "questionable reporters."

To modify a dictionary:

1. Choose Bluebook or California from the search category on the Main menu.

2. Then go to the Activity category and select Modify Dictionary from beneath the CheckCite Action option.

3. Select Go.

4. Choose B to add a case name abbreviation or A to add anything else.

5. Follow on-screen prompts to make the modification.

6. Press Enter to return to the Modify screen.

7. Return to Step 4 to make another modification, or press Esc and Y to exit (unless you know you made a mistake in entering your modifications, in which case you should type N and start over).

Avoiding CheckCite Disasters

Always check to be sure that

1. All the citations in your document really do get checked.

2. The citations checked are the correct citations and not cheap typographical knockoffs.

3. You pay attention to the list of citations to questionable reporters displayed by CheckCite before going on-line. These cites cannot be verified by CheckCite without modification (to them or the dictionary).

Saving Money and Time

THIS CHAPTER COVERS:

Choosing the right subscription(s)

LEXIS versus the books

The Cost command

Savings tips

IT IS POSSIBLE to spend an absolutely stunning amount of money on LEXIS. The opportunities for waste are nearly boundless. However, with a little forethought and careful use, LEXIS can actually save you a lot of money over researching in books. Your savings will vary considerably depending on how efficiently you use the system and on what sort of library you have access to (how far away it is, how complete, and whether you have to pay to maintain it). This chapter focuses on money-saving approaches to using LEXIS.

Choosing the Right Subscription(s)

LEXIS offers a variety of subscriptions and pricing schemes. Choosing the one best suited to your needs can result in substantial savings. Pricing arrangements change frequently, so ask your LEXIS representative what's new, but as of this writing you have five pricing choices:

1. Hourly pricing. You are charged a lot for on-line time (the charge depends on what file you are searching) but pay no per-search charges. This is a good choice if you do a lot of little searches and hardly any on-line reading.

2. Zero-connect pricing. You pay a flat rate per search and then take all the time you want to modify and read results on-line. This saves you the discomfort of big, hairy connect charges breathing down your neck while you try to go faster, faster . . . but it costs a lot unless you are planning to do a lot of reading and cogitating on-line.

3. Transactional pricing. This is the "standard" pricing plan. You pay per search ($7 less per search than the zero-connect rates) plus on-line time ($0.77 per minute; $1.33 to $7.42 less per minute than the "hourly" plan rate). You can save money, but it is more difficult to form strategies (with zero-connect you try to minimize searches and don't worry about anything else, while with hourly you try to minimize on-line time and don't worry about anything else. With transactional, you worry about time and searches. You might rather have less stress and more certainty than the possible savings here. Blood pressure medication isn't cheap either. But maybe you are a with-it, coping, 90s, fast-lane kind of searcher. This could be your thriftiest choice.

4. Project-based pricing. You choose hourly, zero-connect, or transactional on a per-project basis. This allows you to select the most advantageous pricing for each particular project, which can be an advantage but is also one more decision to deal with each time you start out on a project. Unless your research style varies a lot, and in a predictable fashion, this might not be worth the hassle to you.

5. MVP pricing. For one flat monthly fee (as low as $95 for a sole practitioner), you can search in the library of your choice (any state library or one of several specialty libraries) as much as you want; there are no connect time or search charges and no on-line print charges (you still pay to print off-line. Odd, isn't it?). You can access any other file at regular prices (pick a plan). This plan is only available to firms with fewer than 10 attorneys.

■ SOME SAMPLE PRICING DIFFERENCES:

	Zero-Connect (per Search)	Hourly (per Minute)	Transactional
File			
MEGA	$95.00	$8.18	$88.00 per search plus $0.77 per minute
Illinois cases	$20.00	$3.85	$27.00 per search plus $0.77 per minute
Service			
Shepard's	$2.75	$3.85	$2.75 per cite
Auto-Cite	$2.75	$3.85	$2.75 per cite
LEXSEE	$4.00	$3.85	$4.00 per cite
LEXSTAT	$4.00	$3.85	$4.00 per cite ■

Which plan is best for you depends a lot on what non-LEXIS resources are available to you. If you have just opened up a solo practice in the bedroom of your mobile home where you have no law books except a few nutshells and an old copy of Black's *Law Dictionary*, you might as well figure you'll be needing to do a lot of reading on-line. MVP (and/or zero-connect if you need more libraries) will be the best deal for you.

If, on the other hand, your office is across the street from a dandy and free state law library, you may not need to do a lot of reading on-line, or even a lot of research on-line, and you can get the cite lists you need most cheaply using hourly pricing. If you aren't sure, go with project-based pricing, at least at first, and keep careful records to see what your researching patterns really are.

LEXIS versus the Books

If you buy your own law books, you know how phenomenally expensive they are getting to be. It isn't just buying them; updating frequently outstrips the original cost of the book within a few years, and then there is the trouble and expense of handling the updates and maintaining space for the whole business. These costs add up enough to make LEXIS charges start to look a little less appalling.

Even if you don't pay anything for the books you use (say you live across the street from a public law library), you can still save money doing some types of research on LEXIS if you consider your time to be worth anything. Some searches can be done far more efficiently on LEXIS than in the books. Books are better suited for other searches, especially lengthy reading (of cases, for example).

No library has as many sources as LEXIS offers on-line. Some things are much easier on-line or are only possible on-line. For example, you might need to find a quotation from a totally unidentified case. You might be able to find it by devoting the next 12 months of your life to skimming through reporter volumes. Or you could look for it on LEXIS in a single minute. Similarly, you might want to read opinions written by a particular judge you will be going before, to see whether said judge might be inclined to laugh in your face if you make the argument you'd like to make. You could leaf through reporters for hours, reading the beginning of each case to see if your judge wrote it, or enter one line on LEXIS and get a cite list. You could also narrow the list to cases on a particular subject, with a few keystrokes versus—what? An afternoon? A week?

If you maintain your own library, you can save a lot of money, space, and upkeep by using LEXIS for your rarely used sources instead of buying them. For very frequently used sources, you'll probably want to own the books, even if you use LEXIS to search them occasionally. For moderately used sources, or new practitioners with no access to a public or group library, the equation is not so clear. It makes sense to look at each law book you consider buying and ask yourself how many times you are likely to use it. Consider the cost per search to use it on-line. (First check that it is available, and add in some connect time charges. It is hard to estimate accurately, but often even a very rough guesstimate will make the right decision clear.) Say you are considering buying a $3,000 set of re-porters for a state other than your own. You figure you will proba-bly use it 20 or 30 times in the next year. If you used LEXSTAT 50 times, it would cost you $250. You could use LEXSTAT 600 times and come out ahead of the cost of your reporter set. Of course, once you pay for the reporter set it is yours to keep, but you pay more for LEXSTAT everytime you use it. Thus, whether it is worth your while to buy the books depends on how often you will use them and whether you have a preference for them. Of course, some very useful materials aren't available on LEXIS at all, and you'll want to have them handy (practitioner's materials and form books often fall into this category).

The Cost Command

While you are on-line, you can get a list of costs for a file you are in by entering .Cost. You get a display showing the search charges, connect time and telecommunications charges, and how much you have spent on each since you signed on. The command .Cost al-lows you to see your client billing information right away rather than waiting for your monthly bill to come. It can also be used to check on how much each search in a file will cost you, but it is much better to check that out in your paper price list before signing on and to plan your research accordingly.

Savings Tips

There are numerous ways to keep your LEXIS bill smaller than the national debt. Twenty-seven of them are listed here.

1. Choose the smallest appropriate file. Smaller files generally cost less to search than larger ones and yield fewer "false hits" for you to waste expensive time wading through. Read the prices and descriptions of files to pick the smallest one that covers your topic or jurisdiction. For example, you could find the third circuit cases you need by searching GENFED MEGA for $95, or by searching just the Third Circuit cases for $27.

2. Don't search a file when you can use a service. Searching a file costs from $24 to $95. Using a service (LEXSTAT, LEXSEE, LINK) costs $4 to $5. So, if you have a citation, don't search for it in a file. Pull it up with a service and save $19 to $91.

3. Plan your searches and contingency approaches before you sign on. This requires a little time and effort before you sign on but saves you a lot of time and grief afterward and can make a huge difference in your bill. Write out what library and file you will use, your initial search query, and modifications for every eventuality (what if your search retrieves too few documents or too many?). Think through all your options as well as you can before you get on-line where every minute is costing you. Such planning makes it easier to take advantage of the SHORT CUT feature (see Chapter 4) and combine searches (see Tip 19).

4. Proofread a search before you enter it. One little typo and your $95 search is down the drain. Read over it before you push the Enter key. If you realize too late that you made a mistake, try to fix it with a modification rather than a new search, to avoid the new search charge.

5. Use SHORT CUT. See Chapter 8.

6. Use FOCUS or MODIFY instead of a new search. See Chapter 4.

7. Use KWIC and FOCUS to browse more quickly. KWIC and FOCUS let you go to specific terms and evaluate the relevance of your documents much more quickly than just paging through. You might look at a cite list first if you are really uncertain about what you've retrieved. Having browsed your results quickly, you can decide whether you need to modify your search and whether to bother printing or downloading what you've found.

8. Use Custom File Selection selectively. You may save money by combining files, but sometimes it actually costs more. It rarely pays to combine fewer than three files. Drag out your price list and look up the relative costs. Chances are you'll be using the same files again and again and eventually you won't have to look it up every time, but you should check periodically to be sure pricing hasn't changed.

9. Use specialized libraries selectively. Specialized libraries have a variety of materials on a given subject. Sometimes you can find all the materials you need in one specialized topical file rather than searching several jurisdictional and source type files. Read library contents carefully to be sure.

10. Use CheckCite software if you have a lot of cites to check. It works well and saves you on-line time. See Chapter 11.

11. If you get lost, sign off and get help. Some of you guys may have trouble with this one; it is the on-line equivalent of stopping to ask for directions. It may go against the grain for you, but at $0.77 a minute, people can change. When you think you are on the interstate but notice that the road is no longer paved, sign off. Have a look at this book, get a cup of coffee, contemplate your navel, or call 1-800-543-6862: it's free, even if your question is *really* dumb.

12. Get all the free training you can get your hands on. Skilled searchers are efficient searchers, with lower LEXIS bills and more time to watch *Three Stooges* marathons or make origami ducks.

13. Practice free of charge in the PRACTICE library. The PRACT library allows you to get familiar with LEXIS without running up a big bill. There are no connect-time charges for the PRACT library, but print and telecommunications charges apply.

14. Use the 800 number. A lot. It makes no sense to bumble around on-line running up a huge bill when there is free help to be had. 1-800-543-6862. They've heard it all before, and the chances are extremely slim that you'll ever come face to face with one of these people, let alone that they will point and say, "That's him! That's the incredibly stupid guy! You'll never believe what he asked me. . . ."

15. Use CAI or TUTOR to learn the system. Type `.ss` for the select service menu and choose CAI (Computer-Assisted Instruction) or TUTOR (a tutorial) to learn how the system works without connect-time charges. Note that print and telecommunications charges do apply and that if you've read this book there won't be a lot of new information here.

16. Choose the right subscription(s) for your needs. See the first section of this chapter.

17. Use the books you have, at least for lengthy reading. It makes no sense to print or read on-line while the book is sitting on the shelf, unless you need only a small section or the shelf is *really* high. On the other hand, do be sure to use KWIC and FOCUS to cut down on unnecessary reading (see Chapter 5).

18. Print and download selectively. Printing or downloading costs 2 dollars a document. That is a lot, especially for printing garbage. Take a minute to review your results to make sure they are worth having. See Tip 7.

19. Combine searches wherever possible. Every time you can modify your search rather than running a new one, you save big money. It is often possible to do this even when the searches are totally unrelated. Suppose you need to search for x W/5 y OR z, and you also need to run a search in the same database for a. You can run the first search and look at your results, and then add OR a as a modification. You can then use FOCUS to look only at the documents containing a. You have achieved the same results as two searches without the expense of a second search charge.

20. Use LOG. This is a biggie. LOG your search results so that you can recall and modify them later rather than doing a new search. Using LOG and generous forethought, you can usually avoid paying for two searches in the same library on the same day. Whenever you have a search in LOG, you can piggyback another search in that same library without an additional search charge by pulling up the old one and modifying it. As explained in Tip 19, it doesn't matter if the subject matter is totally unrelated; just throw it in with your old search (by modifying) and then use FOCUS to single out the new stuff you need.

21. Use table of contents files and LEXSTAT to find state statutes. If you need to locate a state statute by subject, you can search the statutes file for it to the tune of dollars waltzing across the phone lines, or you can search the state's statutory table of contents file (in the CODES library) for $4 and use LEXSTAT to pull up the section you need (another $4). Use the browsing feature to see adjacent sections if you like (see Chapter 5).

22. Use Segment searches where possible. Segment searching yields more precise results, saving you the expense of weeding irrelevant documents out of your results. Most (not all) searches can be limited to a particular segment with good results (see Chapter 4). This is especially true in NEXIS files, where it is often necessary to limit your search to the Headline and Date segments to avoid retrieving a prohibitively large number of irrelevant or marginally relevant documents.

23. For regular updates of a search, use ECLIPSE. It costs less per search to update using ECLIPSE than to run a new search. See Chapter 8.

24. Consider buying a faster modem. A 9600-baud modem is eight times faster than a 1200-baud modem. Telecommunications and connect-time charges may be costing you more than $0.77 a minute, depending on your subscription plan: if you spend a lot of time online, a new modem could pay for itself fairly quickly. In addition to on-line and connect time, you save *your* time, no longer spent watching screens scroll slowly into and out of existence.

25. *Keep records of your searches and results.* You may be able to avoid repeating searches—and repeating mistakes. Keeping records also helps with billing. When your client wants to know what the #@*! you did on LEXIS that cost him *that much,* you can show him (obviously it is only prudent to research frugally, whether you expect to be called on the carpet or not, and always to wear protective headgear when presenting large bills).

26. *Analyze your bill carefully.* Once you see your LEXIS use patterns on paper, you may see search mistakes you could avoid, inefficient approaches you habitually use, or searches that are just plain not yours (LEXIS passwords are subject to pirating, like anything else, and LEXIS bills are subject to occasional error, like any other bills). Careful consideration of past bills is probably the best way to predict future use and whether a different subscription plan might be better. You may want to periodically reinvestigate whether LEXIS's competitor Westlaw could offer you a better deal. You are in a much better position to decide what system and billing plan is best for you if you have accumulated information about your pattern of usage. LEXIS bills are a little like dieting logs: you may be very surprised at what you actually ate when you see it written down.

27. *Don't forget to enter a client ID.* The cost of research sessions for unidentified clients cannot be billed to the client and contributes to firm overhead costs of lethal proportions. If you or someone in your firm has a seemingly eradicable habit of skipping the client ID, ask LEXIS to rig the system so they can't log in without one. Or, alternatively, post last month's LEXIS bill prominently, with the amount you were unable to bill to clients written in large red print. Hide any sharp objects and be sure all members of the firm know CPR before attempting this maneuver.

CHAPTER 12.   QUICK REFERENCE PAGE

SAVINGS TIPS

1. Choose the smallest appropriate file.
2. Don't search a file when you can use a service.
3. Plan your searches and contingency approaches before you sign on.
4. Proofread a search before you enter it.
5. Use SHORT CUT.
6. Use FOCUS or MODIFY instead of a new search.
7. Use KWIC and FOCUS to browse quickly and avoid unnecessary printing charges.
8. Use Custom File Selection selectively.
9. Use specialized libraries selectively.
10. Use CheckCite software if you have a lot of cites to check.
11. If you get lost, sign off and get help.
12. Get all the free training you can get your hands on.
13. Practice free of charge in the Practice library.
14. Use the 800 number.
15. Use CAI or TUTOR to learn the system.
16. Choose the right subscription(s) for your needs.
17. Use the books you have, at least for lengthy reading.
18. Print and download selectively.
19. Combine searches wherever possible.
20. Use LOG.
21. Use table of contents files and LEXSTAT to find state statutes.
22. Use segment searches where possible.
23. For regular updates of a search, use ECLIPSE.
24. Consider buying a faster modem.
25. Keep records of your searches and results.
26. Analyze your bill carefully.
27. Don't forget to enter a client ID.

Sample Searches

TO RETRIEVE	ENTER
Cases	
by name	name(smith and jones)
by one party's name	name(smith)
by citation	lexsee 445 p2d 902
by subject	restraint w/3 trade
written by a particular judge	writtenby(scalia)
by docket number	91-43543
by a quotation from it	"the law is an ass"
citing a code section	10011
Statutes	
by citation	lexstat 42 usc 1983
by subject	cannabis and possession
a public law	lexsee 100 pl 113
Federal Regulations	
by citation	lexstat 17 cfr 230.146
on a subject	student loan and repay!
Constitutional provisions	
by citation	lexstat uscs const amend 1
by subject	bear arms

(continued)

TO RETRIEVE	ENTER

Law Review Articles

by citation	lexsee 50 ncl 1
by title	to tort or not to tort
by author	Bertha w/3 McGillicudy
about a subject	tort reform
by part of the title	a funny thing happened

An ALR Annotation

by title	title(search and seizure rights of the accused)
by subject	intentional infliction w/10 emotional distress

News

events in the news (search NEWS/CURNWS)	marcia w/2 clark! w/15 hairstyle
NPR transcripts	post office and fire
dishwasher ratings	dishwasher w/10(best or rate!)

Company Information

patents held by a company (search PATENT;ALL)	assignee(sony)
earnings projections (search COMPNY;EARN)	name(reynolds)
information on medical device manufacturers (search GENMED;FDC)	silicone w/15 implant!

Accounting Information

reports on companies with an SIC code (search NAARS;AR)	Sic=102

TO RETRIEVE	ENTER
annual reports (search NAARS;AR)	co(reynolds)
Expert Witnesses	
(search LEXREF:EXPERT)	specialty(pediatrics)
Supreme Court Briefs	
(search GENFED;BRIEFS)	
by subject	best interests w/15 child!
by docket number	87–1011
by names of parties	name(roe and wade)

RESTRICTING A SEARCH BY DATE	EXAMPLE
on a day	dogs and date is April 1, 1992
before a day	dogs and date bef April 1, 1992
before a year	dogs and date bef 1992
after a day	dogs and date aft April 1, 1992
in a date range	dogs and date aft 1992 and date bef 1995
outside a range	dogs and date bef 1992 and date aft 1994

B

Stop Words

ALL	HENCE	SAID	THUS
ALSO	HER	SHE	TO
AM	HERE	SHOULD	TOO
AN	HEREBY	SO	UNTO
AND	HEREIN	SOME	US
ANY	HEREOF	SUCH	VERY
ARE	HEREON	THAN	VIZ
AS	HERETO	THAT	WAS
AT	HEREWITH	THE	WE
BE	HIM	THEIR	WERE
BECAUSE	HIS	THEM	WHAT
BEEN	HOWEVER	THEN	WHEN
COULD	I.E.	THERE	WHERE
DID	IF	THEREBY	WHEREBY
DO	IS	THEREFORE	WHEREIN
DOES	IT	THEREFROM	WHETHER
E.G.	ITS	THEREIN	WHICH
EVER	ME	THEREOF	WHO
FROM	NOR	THEREON	WHOM
HAD	OF	THERETO	WHOSE
HARDLY	ON	THEREWITH	WHY
HAS	ONTO	THESE	WITH
HAVE	OR	THEY	WOULD
HAVING	OUR	THIS	YOU
HE	REALLY	THOSE	

Equivalents

Numeric Equivalents

The numerals 1–20, 30, 40, 50, 60, 70, 80, and 90 automatically retrieve their written equivalents (one, two, etc.), but other numerals (21, 39, etc.) do not. Go figure. The ordinal versions of these same numbers (1st, 2d, etc.) also retrieve their written equivalents (first, second, etc.).

Days of the Week

Monday = Mon   Friday = Fri

Tuesday = Tue   Saturday = Sat

Wednesday = Wed   Sunday = Sun

Thursday = Thur

Months

January = Jan   July = July

February = Feb or Febr   August = Aug

March = Mar   September = Sep or Sept

April = Apr   October = Oct

May = May   November = Nov

June = Jun   December = Dec

States

Alabama = Ala	Maryland = Md
Alaska = Alas	Michigan = Mich
Arizona = Ariz	Minnesota = Minn
Arkansas = Ark	Missouri = Mo
California = Calif or Cal	Montana = Mont
Colorado = Colo	Nebraska = Neb
Connecticut = Conn	Nevada = Nev
Dakota = Dak	New York = NY
Delaware = Del	Oklahoma = Okla
Florida = Fla	Pennsylvania = Pa
Georgia = Ga	Tennessee = Ten or Tenn
Indiana = Ind	Vermont = Vt
Kansas = Kan	Virginia = Va
Kentucky = Ky	Wisconsin = Wis
Louisiana = La	Wyoming = Wyo

Abbreviations of Legal Terms, Names, and Parts of Books

A.D. = AD	AMENDED = AMD
A.E.C. = AEC	AMENDING = AMG
A.G. = AG	ANONYMOUS = ANON
A.L.R. = ALR	APPENDICES = APPENDIX
A.R.R. = ARR	AVENUE = AVE
AFF'D = AFFD	B.F.P. = BFP
AFFG = AFF'G	B.T.A. = BTA

C.A. = CA

C.B. = CB

C.C.A. = CCA

C.C.P.A. = CCPA

C.F.R. = CFR

C.I.A. = CIA

C.I.F. = CIF

C.O.D. = COD

C.P.A. = CPA

C.P.L. = CPL

C.P.L.R. = CPLR

CERTIORARI = CERT

CHAPTER = CH

CIRCUIT = CIR

D.O.D. = DOD

D.O.T. = DOT

E.O. = EO

E.P.T.L. = EPTL

EFFECTIVE = EFF

EXHIBIT = EXH

F = FED

F.A.A. = FAA

F.A.A.A. = FAAA

F.B.I. = FBI

F.C.C. = FCC

F.D.A. = FDA

F.D.I.C. = FDIC

F.I.C.A. = FICA

F.M.C. = FMC

F.O.B. = FOB

F.P.C. = FPC

F.R. = FR

F.R.D. = FRD

F.T.C. = FTC

G.C.M. = GCM

H.E.W. = HEW

H.U.D. = HUD

I.C.C. = ICC

I.R.B. = IRB

I.R.C. = IRC

I.R.S. = IRS

INDICES = INDEX

L.B. = LB

M.T. = MT

MANUSCRIPT = MS

MATRICES = MATRIX

MEMORANDA = MEMO

MIMEOGRAPH = MIM

MOTION = MOT

N.A.S.A. = NASA

N.L.R.B. = NLRB

O.D. = OD

O.E.O. = OEO

P.L. = PL

PARAGRAPH = PARA

PERMANENT = PERM

POUND = LBS

R.S. = RS

REGULATION = REG

REHEARING = REH

REVERSED = REVD OR
     REV'D

REVERSING = REVG OR
     REV'G

S.C.A. = SCA

S.C.P.A. = SCPA

S.M. = SM

S.P.R. = SPR

S.S.T. = SST
SECTION = SEC OR §
SUBDIVISION = SUBD OR
    SUBDIV
SUBSECTION = SUBSEC OR
    §§
SUPPLEMENT = SUPP
T.C. = TC
T.C.M. = TCM
T.D. = TD
T.I.R. = TIR

TEMPORARY = TEMP
TITLE = TIT
TREASURY = TREA
U.C.C. = UCC
U.S.C. = USC
U.S.C.A. = USCA
U.S.C.M.A. = USCMA
VERTICES = VERTEX
VOLUME = VOL
WILLFUL = WILFUL

LEXSEE Abbreviations

A

A	Atlantic Reporter
A2d	Atlantic Reporter, 2d series
AD	New York Appellate Division Reports
AD2d	New York Appellate Division Reports, 2d series
AFTR (P-H)	American Federal Tax Reporter (P-H)
AFTR2d (P-H)	American Federal Tax Reporter (P-H), 2d series
AJIL	American Journal of International Law
ALR	American Law Reports
ALR Fed	American Law Reports, Federal series
ALR2d	American Law Reports, 2d series
ALR3d	American Law Reports, 3d series
ALR4th	American Law Reports, 4th series
ALR5th	American Law Reports, 5th series
Abb	Abbott's U.S. Circuit & District Court Reports
Abb Adm	Abbott's Admiralty Reports
Admin LJ Am U	Administrative Law Journal American University
AGBCA LEXIS	Agriculture Board of Contract Appeals LEXIS cite
Ak ALS	Alaska Advance Legislative Service
Ak Ch	Alaska Chapter
Ak HB	Alaska House Bill
Ak HR	Alaska House Resolution
Ak RESOLVE	Alaska Resolve
Ak SB	Alaska Senate Bill
Ak SR	Alaska Senate Resolution

Al Act	Alabama Acts
Al ALS	Alabama Advance Legislative Service
Al HB	Alabama House Bill
Al HJR	Alabama House Joint Resolution
Al HR	Alabama House Report
Al Pub Act	Alabama Public Act
Al SB	Alabama Senate Bill
Al SJR	Alabama Senate Joint Resolution
Al SR	Alabama Senate Report
Ala	Alabama Reports
Ala Acts	Alabama Acts
Ala AG LEXIS	Alabama Attorney General Opinions LEXIS cite
Ala App	Alabama Appellate Court Reports
Ala App LEXIS	Alabama Appellate Court Opinions LEXIS cite
Ala Civ App LEXIS	Alabama Civil Appellate Opinions LEXIS cite
Ala Crim App LEXIS	Alabama Criminal Appellate Opinions LEXIS cite
Ala LEXIS	Alabama Supreme Court Opinions LEXIS cite
Ala L Rev	Alabama Law Journal
Ala Sec LEXIS	Alabama Securities LEXIS cite
Ala Sec No-Act LEXIS	Alabama No Action Securities LEXIS cite
Ala Tax LEXIS	Alabama Tax LEXIS cite
Alas AG LEXIS	Alaska Attorney General Opinions LEXIS cite
Alas App LEXIS	Alaska Court of Appeals LEXIS cite
Alas LEXIS	Alaska Supreme Court LEXIS cite
Alas Tax LEXIS	Alaska Tax LEXIS cite
Alaska	Alaska Reports
Alaska Sess Laws	Alaska Session Laws
Alb L Rev	Albany Law Review
Am Bank LJ	American Bankruptcy Law Journal
Am Bankr Inst L Rev	American Bankruptcy Institute Law Review
Am Disabilities Dec	American Disabilities Decisions

Am J L and Med	American Journal of Law and Medicine
Am Lab Cas	American Labor Cases (P-H)
Am Law Reg	American Law Register
Am UJ Int'l L & Pol'y	American University Journal of International Law and Policy
Am UL Rev	American University Law Review
AMC	American Maritime Cases
AOD LEXIS	Action on Decisions LEXIS cite
App DC	Appeals Cases, District of Columbia
Ariz	Arizona Reports
Ariz 1st Sp Sess Ch	Arizona 1st Special Session Chapter
Ariz 1st Sp Sess HB	Arizona 1st Special Session House Bill
Ariz 1st Sp Sess SB	Arizona 1st Special Session Senate Bill
Ariz Adv Rep	Arizona Advance Reporter
Ariz AG LEXIS	Arizona Attorney General Opinions LEXIS cite
Ariz ALS	Arizona Advance Legislative Service
Ariz ALS 1st Sp Sess	Arizona ALS 1st Special Session
Ariz ALS 2d Sp Sess	Arizona ALS 2d Special Session
Ariz App.	Arizona Appeals Reports
Ariz App LEXIS	Arizona Appeals Opinions LEXIS cite
Ariz Ch	Arizona Chapter
Ariz HB	Arizona House Bill
Ariz HCM	Arizona House Concurrent Memorial
Ariz L Rev	Arizona Law Review
Ariz LEXIS	Arizona Supreme Court LEXIS cite
Ariz SB	Arizona Senate Bill
Ariz Sec LEXIS	Arizona Securities LEXIS cite
Ariz Sess	Arizona Session Laws
Ariz Tax LEXIS	Arizona Tax LEXIS cite
Ark	Arkansas Reports
Ark Acts	Arkansas Acts
Ark Adv Op	Arkansas Advance Opinions

Ark AG LEXIS	Arkansas Attorney General Opinions LEXIS cite
Ark ALS	Arkansas Advance Legislative Service
Ark ALS (1st Extra Sess)	Arkansas Advance Legislative Service (1st Extra Session)
Ark ALS (2d Extra Sess)	Arkansas Advance Legislative Service (2d Extra Session)
Ark ALS (3d Extra Sess)	Arkansas Advance Legislative Service (3d Extra Session)
Ark App	Arkansas Appellate Reports
Ark App LEXIS	Arkansas Appellate Opinions LEXIS cite
Ark HB	Arkansas House Bill
Ark L Rev	Arkansas Law Review
Ark LEXIS	Arkansas Supreme Court Opinions LEXIS cite
Ark SB	Arkansas Senate Bills
ASBCA LEXIS	Armed Services Board of Contract Appeals Opinions LEXIS cite
AUST MTCT LEXIS	Australia Administrative Appeals Tribunal Opinions LEXIS cite
AUST ACTSC LEXIS	Supreme Court of Australian Capital Territory Opinions LEXIS cite
AUST FAMCT LEXIS	Family Court of Australia LEXIS cite
AUST FEDCT LEXIS	Federal Court of Australia LEXIS cite
AUST HIGHCT LEXIS	High Court of Australia LEXIS cite
AUST IRTCT LEXIS	Australian Immigration Review Tribunal LEXIS cite
AUST NTSC LEXIS	Supreme Court of Northern Territory LEXIS cite (Australia)
AUST SASC LEXIS	Supreme Court of South Australia LEXIS cite
AUST TASSC LEXIS	Supreme Court of Tasmania LEXIS cite (Australia)
Auto Cas (CCH)	Automobile Insurance Cases (CCH)
Auto Cas 2d (CCH)	Automobile Insurance Cases (CCH), 2d series
Av Cas (CCH)	Aviation Cases (CCH)

B

B C Envtl Aff L Rev	Boston College Environmental Affairs Law Review
BC L Rev	Boston College Law Review
BCA (CCH)	Board of Contract Appeals (CCH)
BDIEL	Basic Documents of International Economic Law
BTA	Board of Tax Appeals
BUL Rev	Boston University Law Review
BU Pub Int LJ	Boston University Public Interest Law Journal
BYUL Rev	Brigham Young University Law Review
BALCA LEXIS	Board of Alien Labor Certification Appeals LEXIS cite
Baldw	Baldwin's US Circuit Court Reports
Bank Dev J	Bankruptcy Developments Journal
Banking LJ	Banking Law Journal
Bankr	Bankruptcy Reporter
Bankr Ct Dec (CRR)	Bankruptcy Court Decisions (CRR)
Bankr Ct Dec 2d (CRR)	Bankruptcy Court Decisions (CRR), 2d series
Bankr L Rep (CCH)	Bankruptcy Law Reporter (CCH)
Bankr LEXIS	Bankruptcy Opinions LEXIS cite
Bankr Lit Man	Bankruptcy Litigation Manual
Baylor L Rev	Baylor Law Review
BDIEL AD LEXIS	Basic Documents of International Economic Law LEXIS cite
Ben	Benedict's District Court Reports (US)
BIA LEXIS	Board of Immigration Appeals LEXIS cite
Bill Tracking HR	House of Representatives federal bill-tracking report
Bill Tracking HR Con Res	House of Representatives Concurrent Resolution federal bill-tracking report
Bill Tracking HRJ Res	House of Representatives Joint Resolution federal bill-tracking report
Bill Tracking HR Res	House of Representatives Resolution federal bill-tracking report

Bill Tracking S	Senate federal bill-tracking report
Bill Tracking S Con Res	Senate Concurrent Resolution federal bill-tracking report
Bill Tracking SJ Res	Senate Joint Resolution federal bill-tracking report
Bill Tracking S Res	Senate Resolution federal bill-tracking report
Biss	Bissell's US Circuit Reports
Black	Black's US Supreme Court Reports
Blatch Prize Cas	Blatchford's Prize Cases
Blatchf	Blatchford's US Circuit Court Reports
BNA IER CAS	Individual Employment Rights Cases (BNA)
Brooklyn L Rev	Brooklyn Law Review
BTA LEXIS	Board of Tax Appeals LEXIS cite

C

CAB	Civil Aeronautics Board Reports
CAD	Customs Appeals Decisions
CB	Cumulative Bulletin
CCC 2d	Canadian Criminal Cases, 2d series
CCC 3d	Canadian Criminal Cases, 3d series
CCPA	Court of Customs & Patent Appeals Reports
CIT	Court of International Trade
CMR	Court Martial Reports
CSR	Missouri Code of State Regulations
CAB LEXIS	Civil Aeronautics Board LEXIS cite
CAFC	Court of Appeals, Federal Circuit
Cal AB	California Administrative Board
Cal ALS	California Advance Legislative Service
Cal ALS Extra Session	California Advance Legislative Service Extra Session
Cal ALS Prop	California Advance Legislative Service Proposition
Cal ALS Rule	California Advance Legislative Service Rules
Cal SB	California Senate Bills

Cal	California Reports
Cal 2d	California Reports, 2d series
Cal 3d	California Reports, 3d series
Cal 3d (Spec Trib Supp)	California Reports, 3d series Special Trib Supplement
Cal 4th	California Reports, 4th series
Cal AG LEXIS	California Attorney General Opinions LEXIS cite
Cal App Supp	California Appellate Reports, Supplement
Cal App 2d	California Appellate Reports, 2d series
Cal App 2d Supp	California Appellate Reports, 2d series Supplement
Cal App 3d	California Appellate Reports, 3d series
Cal App 3d Supp	California Appellate Reports, 3d series Supplement
Cal App 4th	California Appellate Reports, 4th series
Cal App 4th Supp	California Appellate Reports, 4th series Supplement
Cal App LEXIS	California Appellate Opinions LEXIS cite
Cal Comp Cas	California Compensation Cases
Cal Daily Op Service	California Daily Opinion Service
Cal ENV LEXIS	California Environmental LEXIS cite
Cal LEXIS	California Supreme Court LEXIS cite
Cal PUC LEXIS	California Public Utilities Commission LEXIS cite
Cal Rptr	California Reporter
Cal Rptr 2d	California Reporter, 2d series
Cal Sec LEXIS	California Department of Corporations LEXIS cite
Cal Tax LEXIS	California Franchise Tax Board & Board of Equalization LEXIS cite
Calif L Rev	California Law Review
Campbell L Rev	Campbell Law Review
Can S Ct LEXIS	Canada Supreme Court LEXIS cite
Cardozo Arts & Ent L J	Cardozo Arts & Entertainment Law Journal

Cardozo L Rev	Cardozo Law Review
Case W Res	Case Western Reserve Law Review
Cath UL Rev	Catholic University Law Review
CCH Prod Liab Rep	Product Liability Reports (CCH)
CFTC LEXIS	Commodity Futures Trading Commission LEXIS cite
Chi-Kent L Rev	Chicago-Kent Law Review
Cl Ct	Claims Court Reporter
Cliff	Clifford's US Circuit Court Reports
CMA LEXIS	Court of Military Appeals LEXIS cite
CMR LEXIS	Court of Military Review LEXIS cite
Collier Bankr Cas (MB)	Collier Bankruptcy Cases (MB)
Collier Bankr Cas 2d (MB)	Collier Bankruptcy Cases (MB), 2d series
Colo	Colorado Reports
Colo 1st Extra Sess HB	Colorado 1st Extra Session House Bill
Colo 1st Extra Sess SB	Colorado 1st Extra Session Senate Bill
Colo AG LEXIS	Colorado Attorney General Opinions LEXIS cite
Colo ALS	Colorado Advance Legislative Service
Colo ALS 1st Extra Sess	Colorado ALS 1st Extra Session
Colo App	Colorado Court of Appeals Reports
Colo App LEXIS	Colorado Court of Appeals LEXIS
Colo Ch	Colorado Chapter
Colo HB	Colorado House Bill
Colo LEXIS	Colorado Supreme Court LEXIS cite
Colo SB	Colorado Senate Bill
Colo Sec LEXIS	Colorado SEC LEXIS cite
Colo Sec No-Act LEXIS	Colorado SEC No Action LEXIS cite
Colo Tax LEXIS	Colorado Tax LEXIS cite
Colum Bus L Rev	Columbia Business Law Review
Colum J Envtl L	Columbia Journal of Environmental Law

Colum L Rev	Columbia Law Review
Comm Fut L Rep (CCH)	Commodity Futures Law Reporter (CCH)
Commr Pat LEXIS	Commissions Decisions Patent & Trademark LEXIS cite
Comp Gen	Decisions of the Comptroller General
Confr Rept	Conference Reports, House of Representatives
Cong Rec D	Congressional Record–Digest
Cong Rec E	Congressional Record–Extension of
Cong Rec H	Congressional Record–House
Cong Rec HL	Congressional Record–House (lobbying)
Cong Rec S	Congressional Record–Senate
Conn	Connecticut Reports
Conn AG LEXIS	Connecticut Attorney General Opinions LEXIS cite
Conn App	Connecticut Appellate Reports
Conn App LEXIS	Connecticut Appellate LEXIS cite
Conn Cir Ct	Connecticut Circuit Court Reports
Conn J Int'l L	Connecticut Journal of International Law
Conn L Rev	Connecticut Law Review
Conn LEXIS	Connecticut Supreme Court LEXIS cite
Conn Op Atty Gen	Connecticut Opinions of the Attorney General
Conn PUC LEXIS	Connecticut Public Utilities Commission LEXIS cite
Conn Sec LEXIS	Connecticut SEC LEXIS cite
Conn Sec No-Act LEXIS	Connecticut SEC No Action LEXIS cite
Conn Super LEXIS	Connecticut Superior Court LEXIS cite
Conn Supp	Connecticut Supplement
Cont Cas Fed (CCH)	Contract Cases Federal (CCH)
Copy L Rep (CCH)	Copyright Law Reporter (CCH)
Cornell Int'l LJ	Cornell International Law Journal
Cornell L Rev	Cornell Law Review
CPIJC	California Public Utilities Commission

CPUC2d	California Public Utilities Commission, 2d series
Creighton L Rev	Creighton Law Review
Ct ALS	Connecticut Advance Legislative Service
Ct CL	Court of Claims
Ct HB	Connecticut House Bill
Ct Intl Trade LEXIS	Court of International Trade LEXIS cite
Conn SB	Connecticut Senate Bill
Cumb L Rev	Cumberland Law Review
Circuit	US Circuit Court Decisions
CUSBUL LEXIS	Customs Bulletin LEXIS cite
Cust B & Dec	Customs Bulletin & Decisions
Cust B & Dec No	Customs Bulletin & Decisions Number
Cust Ct	Customs Court Decisions

D

DC	District of Columbia Reports
DC Act	District of Columbia Acts
DC ALS	District of Columbia Advance Legislative Service
DC Stat	District of Columbia Statutes at Large
DC App LEXIS	District of Columbia Appeals Court LEXIS cite
DC Law	District of Columbia Laws
DLR 2d	Dominion Law Reports, 2d series (Canada)
DLR 3d	Dominion Law Reports, 3d series (Canada)
DLR 4th	Dominion Law Reports, 4th series (Canada)
Daily Journal DAR	Daily Journal DAR (California)
Dall	Dallas' Reports (PA)
Day	Day's Reports (CT)
Dayton L Rev	University of Dayton Law Review
DE AG LEXIS	Delaware Attorney General Opinions LEXIS cite
Del	Delaware Reports
Del ALS	Delaware Advance Legislative Service
Del Ch	Delaware Chancery Reports

Del Ch LEXIS	Delaware Chancery LEXIS cite
Del HB	Delaware House Bill
Del HJR	Delaware House Joint Resolution
Del J Corp L	Delaware Journal of Corporate Law
Del Laws	Delaware Laws
Del LEXIS	Delaware Supreme Court LEXIS cite
Del PSC LEXIS	Delaware Public Service Commission LEXIS cite
Del SB	Delaware Senate Bills
Del Sec No-Act LEXIS	Delaware SEC No Action LEXIS cite
Del SJR	Delaware Senate Joint Resolution
Del Super LEXIS	Delaware Superior Court LEXIS cite
Del Tax LEXIS	Delaware Tax LEXIS cite
Denv UL Rev	Denver University Law Review
DePaul L Rev	DePaul Law Review
DePaul Bus LJ	DePaul Business Law Journal
DOL BCA LEXIS	Department of Labor Board of Contract Appeals LEXIS cite
DOT Av LEXIS	Department of Transportation, Aviation LEXIS cite
DOT BCA LEXIS	Department of Transportation, Board of Contract Appeals LEXIS cite
Duke J Comp & Intl L	Duke Journal of Comparative & International Law
Duke LJ	Duke Law Journal
Duq L Rev	Duquesne Law Review
E	
EBC	Employee Benefit Cases
EBCA LEXIS	Department of Energy Board of Contract Appeals LEXIS cite
EEOC LEXIS	EEOC LEXIS cite
ELR Pend Lit	Environmental Law Reporter, Pending Litigation
ELR Reg	Environmental Law Reporter, Regulations

ELR Stat	Environmental Law Reporter, Statutes
Emory LJ	Emory Law Journal
Emory Int'l L Rev	Emory International Law Review
Empl Pract Dec (CCH)	Employee Practice Decisions (CCH)
Empl Rel	Employee Relations
Empl Rel Appx	Employee Relations Appendix
Enacted HR	House of Representatives—federal bill—enacted version of bill
Enacted HR Con Res	House of Representatives Concurrent Resolution—federal bill—enacted version of bill
Enacted HRJ Res	House of Representatives Joint Resolution—federal bill—enacted version of bill
Enacted HR Res	House of Representatives Resolution—federal bill—enacted version of bill
Enacted S	Senate—federal bill—enacted version of bill
Enacted S Con Res	Senate Concurrent Resolution—federal bill—enacted version of bill
Enacted SJ Res	Senate Joint Resolution—federal bill—enacted version of bill
Enacted S Res	Senate Resolution—federal bill—enacted version of bill
Energy LJ	Energy Law Journal
Eng BCA LEXIS	Corps of Engineers Board of Contract Appeals LEXIS cite
Envtl L	Environmental Law
ERC (BNA)	Environmental Reporter Cases (BNA)

F

F	Federal Reporter
F Cas	Federal Cases
F Supp	Federal Supplement
F2d	Federal Reporter, 2d series
F3d	Federal Reporter, 3d series
FCC	Federal Communications Commission

FCC2d	Federal Communications Commission, 2d series
FERC	Federal Energy Regulatory Commission
FLRA	Federal Labor Relations Authority Decisions
FSIP	Federal Service Impasses Panel
FLRA ALJ Dec No	Federal Labor Relations Authority Decision Number
FPC	Federal Power Commission Reports
FRD	Federal Rules Decisions
FSIP No	Federal Service Impasses Panel Number
FTC	Federal Trade Commission Decisions
Fair Empl Prac Cas (BNA)	Fair Employment Practice Cases (BNA)
FCC LEXIS	Federal Communications Commission LEXIS cite
FCC Rcd	Federal Communications Commission Record
FED App	Federal Appellate (Electronic cite for 6th Circuit)
Fed Banking L Rep (CCH)	Federal Banking Law Reporter (CCH)
Fed Carr Cas (CCH)	Federal Carrier Cases (CCH)
Fed Cir Tr	Federal Circuit Trade Cases
Fed Cl	Federal Claims Court
Fed Com LJ	Federal Communications Law Journal
Fed R Serv (Callaghan)	Federal Rules Service (Callaghan)
Fed R Serv 2d (Callaghan)	Federal Rules Service (Callaghan), 2d series
Fed R Serv 3d (Callaghan)	Federal Rules Service (Callaghan), 3d series
Fed Sec L Rep (CCH)	Federal Securities Law Reporter (CCH)
Fed Sent R	Federal Sentencing Reporter
FERC LEXIS	Federal Energy Regulatory Commission LEXIS cite
Fire & Casualty Cas (CCH)	Fire & Casualty Cases (CCH)
FL ALS	Florida Advance Legislative Service

Fla	Florida Reports
Fla AG LEXIS	Florida Attorney General Opinions
Fla App LEXIS	Florida Appellate LEXIS cite
Fla ENV LEXIS	Florida Environmental LEXIS cite
Fla HB	Florida House Bill
Fla L Rev	Florida Law Review
Fla Law W	Florida Law Weekly
Fla Law WD	Florida Law Weekly District
Fla Law W Fed S	Florida Law Weekly Federal US Supreme Court
Fla Law WS	Florida Law Weekly Supreme Court
Fla Laws Ch	Florida Laws Chapter
Fla LEXIS	Florida Supreme Court LEXIS cite
Fla PUC LEXIS	Florida Public Utilities Commission LEXIS cite
Fla SB	Florida Senate Bills
Fla Sec LEXIS	Florida SEC LEXIS cite
Fla SUL Rev	Florida State University Law Review
Fla Supp	Florida Supplement
Fla Tax LEXIS	Florida Tax LEXIS cite
Flip	Flippin's Circuit Court Reports (US)
FLJ (Title) TOC I	Florida Jurisprudence
FLRA LEXIS	Federal Labor Relations Authority LEXIS cite
FLRA No	Federal Labor Relations Authority Number
Fordham Int'l LJ	Fordham International Law Journal
Fordham L Rev	Fordham Law Review
Fordham Urb LJ	Fordham Urban Law Journal
FPC LEXIS	Federal Power Commission LEXIS cite
FPER (LRP)	Florida Public Employee Reporter (LRP)
FPER (LRP) LEXIS	Florida Public Employee Reporter (LRP) LEXIS cite
FPSC	Florida Public Service Commission
FR	Federal Register

FSIP LEXIS	Federal Service Impasses Panel LEXIS cite
FSIP Rep No	Federal Service Impasses Panel Report Number
FTC LEXIS	Federal Trade Commission LEXIS cite

G

GCM	General Council Memorandum
Ga	Georgia Reports
Ga Act	Georgia Acts
Ga AG LEXIS	Georgia Attorney General Opinions LEXIS cite
Ga ALS	Georgia Advance Legislative Service
Ga ALS (Extra Sess)	Georgia Advance Legislative Service Extra Session
Ga App	Georgia Appeals Reports
Ga App LEXIS	Georgia Appeals LEXIS cite
Ga ENV LEXIS	Georgia Environmental LEXIS cite
Ga HB	Georgia House Bill
Ga HB (Extra Sess)	Georgia House Bill (Extra Session)
Ga HJR	Georgia House Joint Resolution
Ga HR	Georgia House Report
Ga L Rev	Georgia Law Review
Ga Laws	Georgia Laws
Ga LEXIS	Georgia Supreme Court LEXIS cite
Ga SB	Georgia Senate Bill
Ga Sec LEXIS	Georgia SEC LEXIS cite
Ga SJR	Georgia Senate Joint Resolution
Ga SR	Georgia Senate Report
Geo Mason Indep L Rev	George Mason Independent Law Review
Geo Wash L Rev	George Washington Law Review
Golden Gate UL Rev	Golden Gate University Law Review
GSBCA LEXIS	General Services Board of Contract Appeals LEXIS cite
GW J Int'l L & Econ	George Washington Journal of International Law & Economics

H

Harv BlackLetter J	Harvard's Black Letter Journal
Harv CR–CL L Rev	Harvard's Civil Rights–Civil Liberties Law Review
Harv Envt L Rev	Harvard's Environmental Law Review
Harv Hum Rgts J	Harvard's Human Rights Journal
Harv Int'l LJ	Harvard's International Law Journal
Harv J Law and Tec	Harvard's Journal of Law and Technology
Harv J on Legis	Harvard's Journal on Legislation
Harv L Rev	Harvard Law Review
Harv Women's LJ	Harvard's Women's Law Journal
Hastings LJ	Hastings Law Journal
Haw	Hawaii Reports
Haw AG LEXIS	Hawaii Attorney General Opinions LEXIS cite
Haw App	Hawaii Appellate Reports
Haw App LEXIS	Hawaii Appellate LEXIS cite
Haw LEXIS	Hawaii Supreme LEXIS cite
Hawaii L Rev	Hawaii Law Review
Hempst	Hempstead's Reports (US)
Hi Act	Hawaii ACTS
Hi ALS	Hawaii Advance Legislative Service
Hi HB	Hawaii House Bills
Hi SB	Hawaii Senate Bills
Hofstra L Rev	Hofstra Law Review
Hous J Int'l L	Houston Journal of International Law
Hous L Rev	Houston Law Review
HOW	Howard's Supreme Court Reports (MS)
HOW LJ	Howard Law Journal
HRB	House of Representatives–federal bill–unenacted version(s) of bill
HR Con Res	House of Representatives Concurrent Resolution–federal bill–unenacted version(s) of bill

HRJ Res	House of Representatives Joint Resolution—federal bill—unenacted version(s) of bill
HR Res	House of Representatives Resolution—federal bill—unenacted version(s) of bill
HUD BCA LEXIS	Housing & Urban Development Board of Contract Appeals LEXIS cite

I

I & N Dec	Immigration & Naturalization Decisions
ICC	Interstate Commerce Commission Reports
ICC 2d	Interstate Commerce Commission Reports, 2d series
ID	Interior Decisions
ID LEXIS	Interior Decisions LEXIS cite
ILM	International Legal Materials
IRB	Internal Revenue Bulletin
IA ALS	Iowa Advance Legislative Service
IA HF	Iowa House File
IA JR	Iowa House Joint Resolution
IA Laws	Iowa Laws
IA Sec LEXIS	Iowa SEC LEXIS cite
IA SF	Iowa Senate File
IA SJR	Iowa Senate Joint Resolution
IAC	Indiana Administrative Code
IBCA LEXIS	Interior Board of Contract Appeals LEXIS cite
IBLA	Interior Board of Land Appeals Decisions
IBLA LEXIS	Interior Board of Land Appeals LEXIS cite
ICC LEXIS	Interstate Commerce Commission LEXIS cite
Id Sec LEXIS	Idaho SEC LEXIS cite
Id Sec No-Ac LEXIS	Idaho SEC No-Action LEXIS cite
Ida AG LEXIS	Idaho Attorney General Opinions LEXIS cite
Ida ALS	Idaho Advance Legislative Service
Ida App LEXIS	Idaho Appellate LEXIS cite

Ida Ch	Idaho Chapter
Ida HB	Idaho House Bills
Ida HCR	Idaho House Concurrent Resolution
Ida HJM	Idaho House Joint Memorial
Ida LEXIS	Idaho Supreme Court LEXIS cite
Ida SB	Idaho Senate Bills
Ida SCR	Idaho Senate Concurrent Resolution
Ida SJM	Idaho Senate Joint Memorial
Idaho Sess Laws	Idaho Session Laws
Ida Tax LEXIS	Idaho Tax LEXIS cite
Idaho	Idaho Reports
Idaho L Rev	Idaho Law Review
Ill Sec LEXIS	Illinois SEC LEXIS cite
Ill	Illinois Reports
Ill 2d	Illinois Reports 2d series
Ill ALS	Illinois Advance Legislative Service
Ill App	Illinois Appellate Court Reports
Ill App (A)	Illinois Appellate Court Reports, Appendix
Ill App 2d	Illinois Appellate Court Reports, 2d series
Ill App 2d (A)	Illinois Appellate Court Reports, Appendix, 2d series
Ill App 3d	Illinois Appellate Court Reports, 3d series
Ill App 3d (A)	Illinois Appellate Court Reports, Appendix, 3d series
Ill App LEXIS	Illinois Appellate Court LEXIS cite
Ill Dec	Illinois Decisions
Ill ENV LEXIS	Illinois Environmental LEXIS cite
Ill HB	Illinois House Bills
Ill Laws	Illinois Laws
Ill LEXIS	Illinois Supreme Court LEXIS cite
Ill PA	Illinois Public Act
Ill PUC LEXIS	Illinois Public Utilities Commission LEXIS cite

Ill SB	Illinois Senate Bills
Ind	Indiana Reports
Ind Acts	Indiana Acts
Ind AG LEXIS	Indiana Attorney General Opinions LEXIS cite
Ind ALS	Indiana Advance Legislative Service
Ind App	Indiana Court of Appeals Reports
Ind App LEXIS	Indiana Appeals LEXIS cite
Ind Dec	Indiana Decisions
Ind HEA	Indiana House Enacted Act
Ind LJ	Indiana Law Journal
Ind LEXIS	Indiana Supreme Court LEXIS cite
Ind PUC LEXIS	Indiana Public Utilities Commission LEXIS cite
Ind Sec LEXIS	Indiana SEC LEXIS cite
Ind Sec No-Act LEXIS	Indiana SEC No Action LEXIS cite
Ind Tax LEXIS	Indiana Tax LEXIS cite
Ins Tax Rev	Insurance Tax Review
Int'l Law	International Lawyer
Iowa	Iowa Reports
Iowa Acts	Iowa Acts
Iowa AG LEXIS	Iowa Attorney General Opinions LEXIS cite
Iowa App LEXIS	Iowa Court of Appeals LEXIS cite
Iowa J Corp L	Iowa Journal of Corporation Law
Iowa L Rev	Iowa Law Review
Iowa Sup LEXIS	Iowa Supreme Court LEXIS cite
Iowa Tax LEXIS	Iowa Tax LEXIS cite
IRB LEXIS	Cumulative Bulletin LEXIS cite
IRS GCM LEXIS	IRS General Council Memorandum LEXIS cite
ITC GCM LEXIS	International Trade Commission General Council Memorandum LEXIS cite
ITC LEXIS	International Trade Commission LEXIS cite

J

J Contemp HL & Poly	Journal of Contemporary Health Law and Policy
J Crim L	Journal of Criminal Law
J INTL L BUS	Journal of International Law & Business
J Legis	Notre Dame Journal of Legislation
JL & Com	Journal of Law & Commerce
JL & TECH	Journal of Law & Technology
J Pharmacy & Law	Journal of Pharmacy & Law

K

Kan	Kansas Reports
Kan AG LEXIS	Kansas Attorney General Opinions LEXIS cite
Kan ALS	Kansas Advance Legislative Service
Kan App	Kansas Court of Appeals Reports
Kan App 2d	Kansas Court of Appeals Reports, 2d series
Kan App LEXIS	Kansas Court of Appeals LEXIS cite
Kan HB	Kansas House Bill
Kan R	Kansas House Concurrent Resolution
Kan L Rev	Kansas Law Review
Kan LEXIS	Kansas Supreme Court LEXIS cite
Kan SB	Kansas Senate Bill
Kan SCR	Kansas Senate Concurrent Resolution
Kan Sec LEXIS	Kansas Securities Exchange Commission LEXIS cite
Kan Sec No-Ac LEXIS	Kansas SEC No Action LEXIS cite
Kan Sess Laws	Session Laws of Kansas
Kan Tax LEXIS	Kansas Tax LEXIS cite
Ky	Kentucky Reports
Ky 1st Extra Sess Ch	Kentucky 1st Extra Session Chapter
Ky 1st Extra Sess HB	Kentucky 1st Extra Session House Bill
Ky 1st Extra Sess HCR	Kentucky 1st Extra Session House Concurrent Resolution
Ky 1st Extra Sess HJR	Kentucky 1st Extra Session House Joint Resolution

Ky 1st Extra Sess SB	Kentucky 1st Extra Session Senate Bill
Ky 1st Extra Sess SCR	Kentucky 1st Extra Session Senate Concurrent Resolution
Ky 1st Extra Sess SJR	Kentucky 1st Extra Session Senate Joint Resolution
Ky Acts	Kentucky Acts
Ky ALS	Kentucky Advance Legislative Service
Ky ALS 1st Extra Sess	Kentucky Advance Legislative Service 1st Extra Session
Ky App LEXIS	Kentucky Court of Appeals LEXIS cite
Ky Ch	Kentucky Chapter
Ky HB	Kentucky House Bill
Ky HCR	Kentucky House Concurrent Resolution
Ky HJR	Kentucky House Joint Resolution
Ky LJ	Kentucky Law Journal
Ky LEXIS	Kentucky Supreme Court LEXIS cite
Ky Op	Kentucky Court of Appeals Reports
Ky Resolution	Kentucky Resolution
Ky SB	Kentucky Senate Bill
Ky SCR	Kentucky Senate Concurrent Resolution
Ky Sec LEXIS	Kentucky Securities Exchange Commission LEXIS cite
Ky SJR	Kentucky Senate Joint Resolution
Ky Tax LEXIS	Kentucky Board of Tax Appeals LEXIS cite

L

L Ed	Lawyers' Edition, Supreme Court Reports
L Ed 2d	Lawyers' Edition, Supreme Court Reports, 2d
LRRM	Labor Relations Reference Manual (BNA)
La	Louisiana Reports
La ACT	Louisiana Acts
La AG LEXIS	Louisiana Attorney General Opinions LEXIS cite
La ALS	Louisiana Advance Legislative Service
La Ann	Louisiana Annual Reports

La App	Louisiana Court of Appeals Reports
La App LEXIS	Louisiana Court of Appeals LEXIS cite
La ES 1 ACT	Louisiana Extraordinary Session 1st Act
La ES 1 HB	Louisiana Extraordinary Session 1st House Bill
La ES 1 SB	Louisiana Extraordinary Session 1st Senate Bill
La ES 2 ACT	Louisiana Extraordinary Session 2d Act House Bill
La ENV LEXIS	Louisiana Environmental LEXIS cite
La HB	Louisiana House Bill
La L Rev	Louisiana Law Review
La LEXIS	Louisiana Supreme Court LEXIS cite
La PUC LEXIS	Louisiana Public Service Commission LEXIS cite
La Resolution	Louisiana Resolution
La SB	Louisiana Senate Bill
La Tax LEXIS	Louisiana Tax LEXIS cite
Lab Arb (BNA)	Labor Arbitration Reports (BNA)
Lab Cas (CCH)	Labor Cases (CCH)
Life Cas (CCH)	Life Health & Accident Insurance Cases (CCH)
Life Cas 2d (CCH)	Life Health & Accident Insurance Cases, 2d series
Low	Lowell's District Court Reports (U.S. Massachusetts District)
Loy LA L Rev	Loyola University of Los Angeles Law Review
Loy U Chi LJ	Loyola University of Chicago Law Journal

M

MCC	Motor Carrier Cases, Interstate Commerce Commission Reports
MJ	Military Justice Reporter
MSPB	Merit Systems Protection Board Decisions
MSPR	Merit Systems Protection Review
MT HCR	Montana House Concurrent Resolution
MT Resolution	Montana Resolution
Mar Law	Maritime Law

Marq L Rev	Marquette Law Review
Marq Sports LJ	Marquette Sports Law Journal
Mass	Massachusetts Reports
Mass AC LEXIS	Massachusetts Attorney General Opinions LEXIS cite
Mass ALS	Massachusetts Advance Legislative Service
Mass Adv Sh	Massachusetts Advanced Sheet
Mass App Ct	Massachusetts Court of Appeals Reports
Mass App Ct Adv Sh	Massachusetts Appellate Court Advance Sheet
Mass App LEXIS	Massachusetts Court of Appeals LEXIS cite
Mass HB	Massachusetts House Bill
Mass LEXIS	Massachusetts Supreme Judicial Court LEXIS cite
Mass BB	Massachusetts Senate Bill
Mass Sec LEXIS	Massachusetts Securities Exchange Commission LEXIS cite
Mass Sec No-Act LEXIS	Massachusetts SEC No Action LEXIS cite
Mass Tax LEXIS	Massachusetts Tax Appeals LEXIS cite
McAll	McAllister's U.S. Circuit Court Reports
MCC LEXIS	Motor Carrier Cases LEXIS cite
McCahon	McCahon's Reports (ICS)
Md	Maryland Reports
Md AG LEXIS	Maryland Attorney General Opinions LEXIS cite
Md App	Maryland Appellate Reports
Md App LEXIS	Maryland Court of Special Appeals LEXIS cite
Md Ch	Maryland Chancery
Md HB	Maryland House Bill
Md L Rev	Maryland Law Review
Md J Int'l L & Trade	Maryland Journal of International Law & Trade
Md Laws	Maryland Laws
Md LEXIS	Maryland Court of Appeals LEXIS cite
Md PSC	Maryland Public Service Commission

Md PSC LEXIS	Maryland Public Service Commission LEXIS cite
Md SB	Maryland Senate Bill
Md Sec No-Act LEXIS	Maryland SEC No-Action LEXIS cite
Md Tax LEXIS	Maryland Tax Court LEXIS cite
Me	Maine Reports
Me AG LEXIS	Maine Attorney General LEXIS cite
Me ALS	Maine Advance Legislative Service
Me Ch	Maine Chapter
Me HP	Maine House Proposal
Me IB	Maine Initiated Bill
Me Laws	Maine Laws
Me LEXIS	Maine Supreme Court LEXIS cite
Me Resolution	Maine Resolution
Me SP	Maine Senate Proposal
Media L Rep	Media Law Reporter (BNA)
Me L Rev	Maine Law Review
Mem St UL Rev	Memphis State University Law Review
Mercer L Rev	Mercer Law Review
Mi ALS	Michigan Advance Legislative Service
Mi HB	Michigan House Bill
Mi Init	Michigan Initiative
Mi PA	Michigan Public Acts
Mi SB	Michigan Senate Bill
Mich App	Michigan Court of Appeals Reports
Mich App LEXIS	Michigan Court of Appeals LEXIS cite
Mich ENV LEXIS	Michigan Environmental LEXIS cite
Mich J Int'l L	Michigan Journal of International Law
Mich L Rev	Michigan Law Review
Mich LEXIS	Michigan Supreme Court LEXIS cite
Mich PSC LEXIS	Michigan Public Service Commission LEXIS cite
Mich Sec LEXIS	Michigan Department of Commerce Corporations & Securities Bureau LEXIS cite

Mich Tax LEXIS	Michigan Tax Tribunals LEXIS cite
Mich Wrk Comp LEXIS	Michigan Worker's Compensation Appeals Board LEXIS cite
Mil L Rev	Military Law Review
Minn	Minnesota Reports
Minn 1st Sp Sess Ch	Minnesota 1st Special Session Chapter
Minn 1st Sp Sess HF No	Minnesota 1st Special Session House File Number
Minn 1st Sp Sess SF No	Minnesota 1st Special Session Senate File Number
Minn AG LEXIS	Minnesota Attorney General LEXIS cite
Minn ALS	Minnesota Advance Legislative Service
Minn ALS 1st Sp Sess	Minnesota Advance Legislative Service 1st Special Session
Minn App LEXIS	Minnesota Court of Appeals LEXIS cite
Minn Chapter Law	Minnesota Chapter Law
Minn HB	Minnesota House Bill
Minn HB No	Minnesota House Bill Number
Minn HF No	Minnesota House File Number
Minn J Global Trade	Minnesota Journal of Global Trade
Minn L Rev	Minnesota Law Review
Minn LEXIS	Minnesota Supreme Court LEXIS cite
Minn PUC LEXIS	Minnesota Public Utilities Commission LEXIS cite
Minn Resolution	Minnesota Resolution
Minn SB	Minnesota Senate Bill
Minn SB No	Minnesota Senate Bill Number
Minn SF No	Minnesota Senate File Number
Minn Tax LEXIS	Minnesota Tax Court LEXIS cite
Misc	New York Miscellaneous Reports
Misc 2d	New York Miscellaneous Reports, 2d series
Miss	Mississippi Reports
Miss AG LEXIS	Mississippi Attorney General LEXIS cite

Miss ALS	Mississippi Advance Legislative Service
Miss HB	Mississippi House Bill
Miss HCR	Mississippi House Concurrent Resolution
Miss HJR	Mississippi House Joint Resolution
Miss LJ	Mississippi Law Journal
Miss Laws	Mississippi Laws
Miss LEXIS	Mississippi Supreme Court LEXIS cite
Miss SB	Mississippi Senate Bill
Miss SCR	Mississippi Senate Concurrent Resolution
Miss SJR	Mississippi Senate Joint Resolution
Mo	Missouri Reports
Mo AG LEXIS	Missouri Attorney General LEXIS cite
Mo ALS	Missouri Advance Legislative Service
Mo App	Missouri Appeals Reports
Mo App LEXIS	Missouri Court of Appeals LEXIS cite
Mo HB	Missouri House Bill
MO HJR	Missouri House Joint Resolution
Mo L Rev	University of Missouri Law Review
MO LAWS	Missouri Laws
Mo LEXIS	Missouri Supreme Court LEXIS cite
Mo PSC (NS)	Missouri Public Service Commission
Mo PSC LEXIS	Missouri Public Service Commission LEXIS cite
Mo SB	Missouri Senate Bill
Mo Sec LEXIS	Missouri Secretary of State Division of Securities LEXIS cite
MO SJR	Missouri Senate Joint Resolution
Miss Tax	Missouri State Tax Administrative
Mo Tax Ltr Rul LEXIS	Missouri Tax Letter Rulings LEXIS cite
Mont	Montana Reports
Mont AG LEXIS	Montana Attorney General LEXIS cite
Mont LEXIS	Montana Supreme Court LEXIS cite
Mont St Rep	Montana State Reporter (MI)

Mont Tax LEXIS	Montana State Tax Appeals Board LEXIS cite
MPER (LRP)	Michigan Public Employee Reporter (LRP)
MPER (LRP) LEXIS	Michigan Public Employee Reporter (LRP) LEXIS cite
MSPB LEXIS	Merit Systems Protection Board LEXIS cite
MT HJR	Montana House Joint Resolution
MT SCR	Montana Senate Concurrent Resolution
MT SJR	Montana Senate Joint Resolution
M L ALS	Montana Advance Legislative Service
Mt ALS Sp Sess	Montana Advance Legislative Service Special Session
Mt Ch	Montana Chapter
Mt HB	Montana House Bill
Mt HR	Montana House Resolution
Mt SB	Montana Senate Bill
Mt Sp Sess Ch	Montana Special Session Chapter
Mt Sp Sess HB	Montana Special Session House Bill
Mt Sp Sess HJR	Montana Special Session House Joint Resolution
Mt Sp Sess HR	Montana Special Session House Resolution
Mt Sp Sess SB	Montana Special Session Senate Bill
Mt Sp Sess SJR	Montana Special Session Senate Joint Resolution
Mt Sp Sess SR	Montana Special Session Senate Resolution

N

N Dak L Rev	North Dakota Law Review
N Ky L Rev	Northern Kentucky Law Review
NC	North Carolina Reports
NC AG LEXIS	North Carolina Attorney General LEXIS cite
NC ALS	North Carolina Advance Legislative Service
NC App	North Carolina Court of Appeals Reports
NC App LEXIS	North Carolina Court of Appeals LEXIS cite
NC Cent LJ	North Carolina Central Law Journal

NC Ch	North Carolina Chapter
NC HB	North Carolina House Bill
NC J Int'l L & Comm Reg	North Carolina Journal of International Law & Commerce Regulations
NC LEXIS	North Carolina Supreme Court LEXIS cite
NC Sess Laws	North Carolina Session Laws
NC Tax LEXIS	North Carolina Tax LEXIS cite
NCL	North Carolina Law Review
ND	North Dakota Reports
ND AG LEXIS	North Dakota Attorney General LEXIS cite
ND ALS	North Dakota Advance Legislative Service
ND App LEXIS	North Dakota Court of Appeals LEXIS cite
ND Ch	North Dakota Chapter
ND HB	North Dakota House Bill
ND HCR	North Dakota House Concurrent Resolution
ND HJR	North Dakota House Joint Resolution
ND HR	North Dakota House Resolution
ND Laws	North Dakota Laws
ND LEXIS	North Dakota Supreme Court LEXIS cite
ND SB	North Dakota Senate Bill
ND SCR	North Dakota Senate Concurrent Resolution
ND SJR	North Dakota Senate Joint Resolution
ND SR	North Dakota Senate Resolution
NE	North Eastern Reporter
NE 2d	North Eastern Reporter, 2d series
NH	New Hampshire Reporter
NH AG LEXIS	New Hampshire Attorney General LEXIS cite
NH HJR	New Hampshire House Joint Resolution
NH LEXIS	New Hampshire Supreme Court LEXIS cite
NH SJR	New Hampshire Senate Joint Resolution
NH Tax LEXIS	New Hampshire Board of Tax & Land Appeals LEXIS cite

NJ	New Jersey Reports
NJ A N	New Jersey Assembly Number
NJ ACR	New Jersey Assembly Concurrent Resolution
NJ AG LEXIS	New Jersey Attorney General LEXIS cite
NJ AJR	New Jersey Assembly Joint Resolution
NJ ALS	New Jersey Advance Legislative Service
NJ Ch	New Jersey Chapter
NJ CR	New Jersey Concurrent Resolution
NJ ENV LEXIS	New Jersey Environmental LEXIS cite
NJ Eq	New Jersey Equity Reports
NJ JR	New Jersey Joint Resolution
NJ Laws	New Jersey Laws
NJ LEXIS	New Jersey Supreme Court LEXIS cite
NJ Misc	New Jersey Miscellaneous Reports
NJ SN	New Jersey Senate Number
NJ SCR	New Jersey Senate Concurrent Resolution
NJ SJR	New Jersey Senate Joint Resolution
NJ Super	New Jersey Superior Court Reports
NJ Super LEXIS	New Jersey Superior Court LEXIS cite
NJ Tax	New Jersey Tax Court Reports
NJ Tax LEXIS	New Jersey Tax Court LEXIS cite
NJAR2d(ABC)	New Jersey Agency Reports 2d series (Alcohol Beverage Control)
NJAR2d(BDS)	New Jersey Agency Reports 2d series (Professional Boards)
NJAR2d(BKG)	New Jersey Agency Reports 2d series (Banking)
NJAR2d(BRC)	New Jersey Agency Reports 2d series (Board of Regulatory Commissioners)
NJAR2d(CAF)	New Jersey Agency Reports 2d series (Community Affairs)
NJAR2d(CCC)	New Jersey Agency Reports 2d series (Casino Control Commission)

NJAR2d(CMA)	New Jersey Agency Reports 2d series (Consumer Affairs)
NJAR2d(CRT)	New Jersey Agency Reports 2d series (Civil Rights)
NJAR2d(CSV)	New Jersey Agency Reports 2d series (Civil Service)
NJAR2d(DEA)	New Jersey Agency Reports 2d series (Division of Economic Assistance)
NJAR2d(DMA)	New Jersey Agency Reports 2d series (Division of Medical Assistance Health Services)
NJAR2d(EDS)	New Jersey Agency Reports 2d series (Special Education)
NJAR2d(EDU)	New Jersey Agency Reports 2d series (Education)
NJAR2d(PC)	New Jersey Agency Reports 2d series (Pinelands Commission)
NJAR2d(EPE)	New Jersey Agency Reports 2d series (Environmental Protection & Energy)
NJAR2d(HED)	New Jersey Agency Reports 2d series (Higher Education)
NJAR2d(HLT)	New Jersey Agency Reports 2d series (Health)
NJAR2d(LBR)	New Jersey Agency Reports 2d series (Labor & Industry)
NJAR2d(MVH)	New Jersey Agency Reports 2d series (Motor Vehicles)
NJAR2d(OAL)	New Jersey Agency Reports 2d series (Office of Administrative Law)
NJAR2d(POL)	New Jersey Agency Reports 2d series (State Police)
NJ AR2d(PTC)	New Jersey Agency Reports 2d series (Police Training Commission)
NJAR2d(RAC)	New Jersey Agency Reports 2d series (Racing Commission)
NJAR2d(REC)	New Jersey Agency Reports 2d series (Real Estate Commission)

NJAR2d(STE)	New Jersey Agency Reports 2d series (State Department)
NJAR2d(TRP)	New Jersey Agency Reports 2d series (Transportation)
NJAR2d(PEN)	New Jersey Agency Reports 2d series (Pensions)
NJAR2d(UCC)	New Jersey Agency Reports 2d series (Unemployment Compensation)
NJL	New Jersey Law Reports
NLRB	National Labor Relations Board Reports
NM	New Mexico Reports
NM AG LEXIS	New Mexico Attorney General LEXIS cite
NM ALS	New Mexico Advance Legislative Service
NM App	New Mexico Court of Appeals
NM App LEXIS	New Mexico Court of Appeals LEXIS cite
NM Ch	New Mexico Chapter
NM HB	New Mexico House Bill
NM Laws	New Mexico Laws
NM LEXIS	New Mexico Supreme Court LEXIS cite
NM SB	New Mexico Senate Bill
NM St B Bull	New Mexico State Bar Bulletin
NM L Rev	New Mexico Law Review
NRC	National Regulatory Commission Issuances
NTSB	National Transportation Safety Board Decisions
NW	North Western Reporter
NW2d	North Western Reporter, 2d series
NY	New York Reports
NY AN	New York Assembly Number
NY AG LEXIS	New York Attorney General LEXIS cite
NY ALS	New York Advance Legislative Service
NY App Div LEXIS	New York Appellate Division LEXIS cite
NY City Tax LEXIS	New York City Tax LEXIS cite
NY Civ Proc Rep (ns)	New York Civil Court Procedures Reporter (n. s.)

NY Comp LEXIS	New York State Comptroller LEXIS cite
NY ENV LEXIS	New York Environmental LEXIS cite
NY Laws	New York Laws
NYJ	New York Jurisprudence
NY LEXIS	New York Supreme Court LEXIS cite
NY Misc LEXIS	New York Miscellaneous LEXIS cite
NY PUC LEXIS	New York Public Service Commission LEXIS cite
NY SN	New York Senate Number
NY ST Comp	New York State Comptroller Decisions
NY Tax LEXIS	New York Tax Commission LEXIS cite
NY2d	New York Reports 2d series
NYS	New York Supplement
NYS2d	New York Supplement 2d series
NYUL Rev	New York University Law Review
NAIC Proc	National Association of Insurance Commissioners Proceedings
NASA BCA LEXIS	NASA Board of Contract Appeals LEXIS cite
Nal Res Tax Rev	Natural Resources Tax Review
NCA	Decisions of the Nebraska Court of Appeals
ND Resolution	North Dakota Resolution
Neb	Nebraska Reports Service
Neb App	Nebraska Appeals
Neb App LEXIS	Nebraska Appeals LEXIS cite
Neb L Rev	Nebraska Law Review
Neb Laws	Nebraska Laws
Neb LB	Nebraska Legislative Bill
Neb LEXIS	Nebraska Supreme Court LEXIS cite
Neb LR	Nebraska Legislative Resolution
Neg Cas (CCH)	Negligence Cases (CCH)
Neg Cas 2d (CCH)	Negligence Cases 2d series (CCH)
Nev	Nevada Reports
Nev AB	Nevada Assembly Bill

Nev Adv Ops No	Nevada Advance Opinion Number
Nev HB	Nevada House Bill
Nev AG LEXIS	Nevada Attorney General LEXIS cite
Nev ALS	Nevada Advance Legislative Service
Nev ALS (Sp Sess)	Nevada Advance Legislative Service (Special Session)
Nev Ch	Nevada Chapter
Nev LEXIS	Nevada Supreme Court LEXIS cite
Nev Resolution	Nevada Resolution
Nev SB	Nevada Senate Bill
New Eng L Rev	New England Law Review
NE J on Crim & Civ C	New England Journal of Criminal & Civil Confinement
Newb Adm	Newberry's District Court Admiralty Reports
NH ALS	New Hampshire Advance Legislative Service
NH Ch	New Hampshire Chapter
NH HB	New Hampshire House Bill
NH LAWS	New Hampshire Laws
NH SB	New Hampshire Senate Bill
NJPER (LRP)	New Jersey Public Employee Reporter (LRP)
NJPER (LRP) LEXIS	New Jersey Public Employee Reporter (LRP) LEXIS cite
NLRB Dec (CCH)	National Labor Relations Board Decisions
NLRB GCM LEXIS	National Labor Relations Board General Counsel Memorandum LEXIS cite
NLRB LEXIS	National Labor Relations Board LEXIS cite
NLRB No	National Labor Relations Board Number
NOAA LEXIS	National Oceanic & Atmospheric Administration LEXIS cite
Notre Dame L Rev	Notre Dame Law Review
NTSB LEXIS	National Transportation Safety Board LEXIS cite

NW UL Rev	Northwestern University Law Review
NY PSC	New York Public Service Commission

O

OBAJ	Oklahoma Bar Association Journal
OCC CB LEXIS	Office of Comptroller of the Currency Cumulative Bulletin LEXIS cite
OCC Enf Dec LEXIS	Office of Comptroller of the Currency Enforcement Decisions LEXIS cite
OCC Ltr LEXIS	Office of the Comptroller of the Currency Letters LEXIS cite
Oh Sec LEXIS	Ohio Securities Exchange Commission LEXIS cite
Ohio	Ohio Reports
Ohio AG LEXIS	Ohio Attorney General LEXIS cite
Ohio App	Ohio Appellate Reports
Ohio App 2d	Ohio Appellate Reports 2d series
Ohio App 3d	Ohio Appellate Reports 3d series
Ohio App LEXIS	Ohio Court of Appeals LEXIS cite
Ohio B Rep	Ohio Bar Association Reports
Ohio ENV LEXIS	Ohio Environmental LEXIS cite
Ohio HB	Ohio House Bill
Ohio HJR	Ohio House Joint Resolution
Ohio L Abs	Ohio Law Abstracts
Ohio L Rep	Ohio Law Reporter
Ohio LEXIS	Ohio Supreme Court LEXIS cite
Ohio Misc	Ohio Miscellaneous Reports
Ohio Misc 2d	Ohio Miscellaneous Reports 2d series
Ohio Misc LEXIS	Ohio Miscellaneous Courts LEXIS cite
Ohio NUL Rev	Ohio Northern University Law Review
Ohio Op	Ohio Opinions
Ohio Op 2d	Ohio Opinions 2d series
Ohio Op 3d	Ohio Opinions 3d series
Ohio PUC LEXIS	Ohio Public Utilities Commission LEXIS cite

Ohio SJR	Ohio Senate Joint Resolution
Ohio SB	Ohio Senate Bill
Ohio St	Ohio State Reports
Ohio St 2d	Ohio State Reports 2d series
Ohio St 3d	Ohio State Reports 3d series
Ohio St LJ	Ohio State Law Journal
Ohio Tax LEXIS	Ohio Board of Tax Appeals LEXIS cite
OHJ (title) TOC I	Ohio Jurisprudence
OK ALS	Oklahoma Advance Legislative Service
OK Ch	Oklahoma Chapter
OK HB	Oklahoma House Bill
OK HCR	Oklahoma House Concurrent Resolution
OK HJR	Oklahoma House Joint Resolution
OK HR	Oklahoma House Resolution
OK RESOLUTION	Oklahoma Resolution
OK SB	Oklahoma Senate Bill
OK SCR	Oklahoma Senate Concurrent Resolution
OK SJR	Oklahoma Senate Joint Resolution
OK SR	Oklahoma Senate Resolution
Okla	Oklahoma Reports
Okla AG LEXIS	Oklahoma Attorney General LEXIS cite
Okla Civ App LEXIS	Oklahoma Court of Civil Appeals LEXIS cite
Okla Crim App LEXIS	Oklahoma Court of Criminal Appeals LEXIS cite
Okla L Rev	Oklahoma Law Review
Okla LEXIS	Oklahoma Supreme Court LEXIS cite
Okla Sec LEXIS	Oklahoma Securities Commission LEXIS cite
Okla Tax LEXIS	Oklahoma Tax Commission LEXIS cite
OLC LEXIS	Office of Legal Counsel LEXIS cite
Op (Inf) Atty Gen Alas	Alaska Attorney General Opinions (Informal)
Op (Inf) Atty Gen NY	New York Attorney General Opinions (Informal)
Op Atty Gen Ala	Alabama Attorney General Opinions

Op Atty Gen Alas No	Alaska Attorney General Opinions (Number)
Op Atty Gen Ariz	Arizona Attorney General Opinions
Op Atty Gen Ark	Arkansas Attorney General Opinions
Op Atty Gen Cal	California Attorney General Opinions
Op Atty Gen Col	Colorado Attorney General Opinions
Op Atty Gen Del	Delaware Attorney General Opinions
Op Atty Gen Fla	Florida Attorney General Opinions
Op Atty Gen Ga	Georgia Attorney General Opinions
Op Atty Gen Hi	Hawaii Attorney General Opinions
Op Atty Gen Idaho	Idaho Attorney General Opinions
Op Atty Gen Ill	Illinois Attorney General Opinions
Op Atty Gen Ind	Indiana Attorney General Opinions
Op Atty Gen Iowa	Iowa Attorney General Opinions
Op Atty Gen Kan	Kansas Attorney General Opinions
Op Atty Gen Ky	Kentucky Attorney General Opinions
Op Atty Gen Ky LEXIS	Kentucky Attorney General Opinions LEXIS cite
Op Atty Gen La	Louisiana Attorney General Opinions
Op Atty Gen Mass	Massachusetts Attorney General Opinions
Op Atty Gen Md	Maryland Attorney General Opinions
Op Atty Gen Me	Maine Attorney General Opinions
Op Atty Gen Mich	Michigan Attorney General Opinions
Op Atty Gen Minn	Minnesota Attorney General Opinions
Op Atty Gen Miss	Mississippi Attorney General Opinions
Op Atty Gen Mo	Missouri Attorney General Opinions
Op Atty Gen Mont	Montana Attorney General Opinions
Op Atty Gen Mont No	Montana Attorney General Opinions (Number)
Op Atty Gen NH	New Hampshire Attorney General Opinions
Op Atty Gen NJ	New Jersey Attorney General Opinions
Op Atty Gen NC	North Carolina Attorney General Opinions
Op Atty Gen ND	North Dakota Attorney General Opinions
Op Atty Gen NM	New Mexico Attorney General Opinions

Op Atty Gen NY	New York Attorney General Opinions
Op Atty Gen Nev	Nevada Attorney General Opinions
Op Atty Gen Ohio	Ohio Attorney General Opinions
Op Atty Gen Okla	Oklahoma Attorney General Opinions
Op Atty Gen Ore	Oregon Attorney General Opinions
Op Atty Gen Pa	Pennsylvania Attorney General Opinions
Op Atty Gen RI	Rhode Island Attorney General Opinions
Op Atty Gen SC	South Carolina Attorney General Opinions
Op Atty Gen SD	South Dakota Attorney General Opinions
Op Atty Gen Tenn	Tennessee Attorney General Opinions
Op Atty Gen Tex	Texas Attorney General Opinions
Op Atty Gen Utah	Utah Attorney General Opinions
Op Atty Gen Va	Virginia Attorney General Opinions
Op Atty Gen WVa	West Virginia Attorney General Opinions
Op Atty Gen Wash	Washington Attorney General Opinions
Op Atty Gen Wash No	Washington Attorney General Opinions (number)
Op Atty Gen Wis	Wisconsin Attorney General Opinions
Op Atty Gen Wyo	Wyoming Attorney General Opinions
Op OLC	Opinions of the Office of Legal Counsel
Op OLC (Vol A)	Opinions of the Office of Legal Counsel (Volume A)
Op OLC (Vol B)	Opinions of the Office of Legal Counsel (Volume B)
Op Sec PRR	Opinions of the Secretary of Public Relations
OPER (LRP)	Ohio Public Employee Reporter (LRP)
OPER (LRP) LEXIS	Ohio Public Employee Reporter (LRP) LEXIS cite
Or L Rev	Oregon Law Review
Ore	Oregon Reports
Ore AG LEXIS	Oregon Attorney General LEXIS cite
Ore ALS	Oregon Advance Legislative Service
Ore App	Oregon Court of Appeals Reports

Ore App LEXIS	Oregon Court of Appeals LEXIS cite
Ore HB	Oregon House Bill
Ore HCR	Oregon House Concurrent Resolution
Ore HJM	Oregon House Joint Memorial
Ore HJR	Oregon House Joint Resolution
Ore Laws	Oregon Laws & Regulations
Ore LEXIS	Oregon Supreme Court LEXIS cite
Ore SB	Oregon Senate Bill
Ore SCR	Oregon Senate Concurrent Resolution
Ore Sec LEXIS	Oregon Securities Commission LEXIS cite
Ore SJM	Oregon Senate Joint Memorial
Ore SJR	Oregon Senate Joint Resolution
Ore Tax LEXIS	Oregon Tax Court LEXIS cite
OSAHRC	Occupational Safety & Health Review Commission
OSAHRC LEXIS	Occupational Safety & Health Review Commission LEXIS cite
OSHC (BNA)	Occupational Safety & Health Cases (BNA)
OSHD (CCH)	Occupational Safety & Health Decisions (CCH)
OTR	Oregon Tax Reports

P

P	Pacific Reporter
P2d	Pacific Reporter 2d series
Pace Envtl L Rev	Pace Environmental Law Review
Pace Int'l L Rev	Pace International Law Review
Pace L Rev	Pace Law Review
PH	Pattent & Health Reports (VA)
PL	Public Laws
PR Sent	Puerto Rico Sentencias
PUR4th	Public Utilities Reports 4th series
Pa	Pennsylvania State Reports
Pa AG LEXIS	Pennsylvania Attorney General LEXIS cite

Pa ALS	Pennsylvania Advance Legislative Service
Pa Commw	Pennsylvania Commonwealth Court Reports
Pa Commw LEXIS	Pennsylvania Commonwealth Court LEXIS cite
Pa Envim LEXIS	Pennsylvania Environmental Hearing Board LEXIS cite
Pa HB	Pennsylvania House Bill
Pa HCR	Pennsylvania House Concurrent Resolution
PA HJR	Pennsylvania House Joint Resolution
Pa Laws	Pennsylvania Laws
Pa LEXIS	Pennsylvania Supreme Court LEXIS cite
Pa PUC	Pennsylvania Public Utilities Commission
Pa PUC LEXIS	Pennsylvania Public Utilities Commission LEXIS cite
Pa SB	Pennsylvania Senate Bill
Pa SCR	Pennsylvania Senate Concurrent Resolution
Pa SJR	Pennsylvania Senate Joint Resolution
Pa Sec LEXIS	Pennsylvania Securities Commission LEXIS cite
Pa Super	Pennsylvania Superior Court Reports
Pa Super LEXIS	Pennsylvania Superior Court LEXIS cite
Pa Tax LEXIS	Pennsylvania Commonwealth Court Tax LEXIS cite
Pat App LEXIS	Board of Patent Appeals & Interferences LEXIS cite
PBGC LEXIS	Pension Benefit Guarantee Corporation LEXIS cite
Pepp L Rev	Pepperdine Law Review
PERC (LRP)	Public Employment Reporter for California
PERC (LRP) LEXIS	Public Employment Reporter for California LEXIS cite
PERI (LRP)	Public Employment Reporter for Illinois
PERI (LRP) LEXIS	Public Employment Reporter for Illinois LEXIS cite
Pet Adm	Peter's District Court Admiralty Reports
Pet CC	Peter's United States Circuit Court Reports

Phila	Philadelphia Reports (PA)
Phila Cty Rptr LEXIS	Philadelphia County Reporter LEXIS cite
PR ACT	Puerto Rico Act
PR ALS	Puerto Rico Advance Legislative Service
PR HB	Puerto Rico House Bill
PR LAWS	Puerto Rico Laws
PR SB	Puerto Rico Senate Bill
PRIVATE RULING	Private Letter Ruling
PRL LEXIS	Private Letter Ruling LEXIS cite
PSBCA LEXIS	Postal Service Board of Contract Appeals LEXIS cite
Pub Lands Dec	United States Land Office Decisions
Pub Lands Rev	Public Lands Revised
Puget Sound L Rev	Puget Sound Law Review

Q

No publications currently available

R

RI	Rhode Island Reports
RI AG LEXIS	Rhode Island Attorney General LEXIS cite
RI ALS	Rhode Island Advance Legislative Service
RI HB	Rhode Island House Bill
RI LEXIS	Rhode Island Supreme Court LEXIS cite
RI Pub Ch	Rhode Island Public Chapter
RI Pub Laws	Rhode Island Public Laws
RI SB	Rhode Island Senate Bill
RI Tax LEXIS	Rhode Island Tax Appeals LEXIS cite
Rad Reg 2d (P & F)	Radio Regulation Reporter 2d series (P & F)
REV PROC	Revenue Procedure
REV RUL	Revenue Ruling
RIAFTC	Research Institute of America Federal Tax

(Each chapter is individually available through the LEXSEE feature by using the following format: reporter abbreviation chapter number section number, i.e., RIAFTC A 1000.)

RICO Bus Disp Guide	RICO Business Dispute Guide
RTC LEXIS	Resolution Trust Corporation LEXIS cite
Rutgers L Rev	Rutgers Law Review

S

S	Senate—federal bill—unenacted version(s) of bill
S Cal L Rev	Southern California Law Review
S Con Res	Senate Concurrent Resolution—federal bill—unenacted version(s) of bill
S Ct	Supreme Court Reporter
S Ill U L J	Southern Illinois University Law Journal
SC	South Carolina Reports
SC ACT	South Carolina Actions and Joint Resolutions
SC AG LEXIS	South Carolina Attorney General LEXIS cite
SC App LEXIS	South Carolina Court of Appeals LEXIS cite
SC HB	South Carolina House Bill
SC L Rev	South Carolina Law Review
SC LEXIS	South Carolina Supreme Court LEXIS cite
SC R	Supreme Court Reporter
SC SB	South Carolina Senate Bill
SC Tax LEXIS	South Carolina Tax Commission LEXIS cite
SD	South Dakota Reporter
SD AG LEXIS	South Dakota Attorney General LEXIS cite
SD ALS	South Dakota Advance Legislative Service
SD CH	South Dakota Chapter
SD HB	South Dakota House Bill
SD L REV	South Dakota Law Review
SD Laws	South Dakota Laws
SD LEXIS	South Dakota Supreme Court LEXIS cite
SD SB	South Dakota Senate Bill
SD Sec No-Act LEXIS	South Dakota Securities No-Action LEXIS cite
SE	South Eastern Reporter

SE 2d	South Eastern Reporter 2d series
SEC	Securities & Exchange Commission Decisions
SJ Res	Senate Joint Resolution—federal bill—unenacted version(s) of bill
S Res	Senate Resolution—federal bill—unenacted version(s) of bill
SW	South Western Reporter
SW2d	South Western Reporter 2d series
San Diego L Rev	San Diego Law Review
SEC Jud Dec	Securities & Exchange Commission Judicial Decisions
SEC LEXIS	Securities & Exchange Commission Decisions LEXIS cite
SEC No-Act LEXIS	Securities & Exchange Commission No-Action LEXIS cite
Seton Hall L Rev	Seton Hall Law Review
Seton Hall Legis J	Seton Hall Legislative Journal
SLIP OP	Slip opinion (Court of International Trade only)
So	Southern Reporter
So 2d	Southern Reporter 2d series
Sprague	Sprague's United States District Court (Admiralty) Decisions
St John's L Rev	St. John's Law Review
St John's JL Comm	St. John's Journal of Legal Community
St Louis LJ	St. Louis Law Journal
St Mary's LJ	St. Mary's Law Journal
Stan Envtl LJ	Stanford Environmental Law Journal
Stan J Int'l L	Stanford Journal of International Law
Stan L Rev	Stanford Law Review
Stat	US Statutes at Large
Stetson L Rev	Stetson Law Review
Suffolk UL Rev	Suffolk University Law Review
Sumn	Sumner's United States Circuit Court Reports

Syracuse J Int'l L & Com	Syracuse Journal of International Law & Commerce
Syracuse L Rev	Syracuse Law Review

T

TC	Tax Count
TC Memo	Tax Court Memorandum Decisions
TC No	Tax Court Number
TCM (CCH)	Tax Court Memorandum Decisions (CCH)
Tc Mem Ph	Tax Court Memorandum (Prentice Hall)
Tax Ct Memo LEXIS	U.S. Tax Court Memorandum LEXIS cite
Tax L Rev	New York University Tax Law Review
Temp Int'l & Comp LJ	Temple International & Comparative Law Journal
Temple L Rev	Temple Law Review
Temple Pol & Civ Rts LR	Temple Political & Civil Rights Law Review
Tenn	Tennessee Reports
Tenn AG LEXIS	Tennessee Attorney General LEXIS cite
Tenn App	Tennessee Appeals
Tenn App LEXIS	Tennessee Court of Appeals LEXIS cite
Tenn Crim App LEXIS	Tennessee Court of Criminal Appeals LEXIS cite
Tenn L Rev	Tennessee Law Review
Tenn LEXIS	Tennessee Supreme Court LEXIS cite
Tenn Pub Acts	Tennessee Public Acts
Tenn Reg LEXIS	Tennessee Regulations LEXIS cite
Tex	Texas Reports
Tex AG LEXIS	Texas Attorney General LEXIS cite
Tex ALS	Texas Advance Legislative Service
Tex App LEXIS	Texas Court of Appeals & Civil Appeals LEXIS cite
Tex Ch	Texas Chapter
Tex Crim	Texas Criminal Reports
Tex Crim App LEXIS	Texas Court of Criminal Appeals LEXIS cite

Tex Gen Laws	Texas General Laws
Tex HB	Texas House Bill
Tex HCR	Texas House Concurrent Resolution
Tex HJR	Texas House Joint Resolution
Tex L Rev	Texas Law Review
Tex LEXIS	Texas Supreme Court LEXIS cite
Tex PUC LEXIS	Texas Public Utilities Commission LEXIS cite
Tex SB	Texas Senate Bill
Tex SCR	Texas Senate Concurrent Resolution
Tex Sec LEXIS	Texas Securities Commission LEXIS cite
Tex SJR	Texas Senate Joint Resolution
Tex Sup J	Texas Supreme Court Journal
Tex Tax LEXIS	Texas Comptroller LEXIS cite
Tex Tech L Rev	Texas Technical Law Review
Texas PUC Bulletin	Texas Public Utilities Commission Bulletins
TM LEXIS	Technical Memorandum LEXIS cite
TMR	The Trademark Reporter
Tn ALS	Tennessee Advance Legislative Service
Tn Pub Ch	Tennessee Public Chapter
Tn SB	Tennessee Senate Bill
Trade Cas (CCH)	Trade Cases (CCH)
Transp L J	Transportation Law Journal
TTAB LEXIS	Trademark Trial & Appeals Board LEXIS cite
Tul Envtl LJ	Tulane Environmental Law Journal
Tul L Rev	Tulane Law Review
TXJ (title) TOC I	Texas Jurisprudence

U

U Ark Little Rock LJ	University of Arkansas–Little Rock Law Journal
U Balt L Rev	University of Baltimore Law Review
U Chi L Rev	University of Chicago Law Review
U Chi Legal F	University of Chicago Legal Forum

U Cin L Rev	University of Cincinnati Law Review
U Colo L Rev	University of Colorado Law Review
U Ill L Rev	University of Illinois Law Review
U Miami L Rev	University of Miami Law Review
U Mich JL	University of Michigan Journal of Law
U Pa J Int'l Bus L	University of Pennsylvania International Business Law
U Pa L Rev	University of Pennsylvania Law Review
U Pitt L Rev	University of Pittsburgh Law Review
U Rich L Rev	University of Richmond Law Review
U Tol L Rev	University of Toledo Law Review
UC Davis L Rev	University of California at Davis Law Review
UCC Rep Serv (Callaghan)	Uniform Commercial Code Reporting Service
UCCR Serv 2d (Callaghan)	Uniform Commercial Code Reporting Service 2d series
US	United States Reports
US AG LEXIS	United States Attorney General LEXIS cite
US App	United States Court of Appeals
US App DC	United States Court of Appeals (DC)
US App LEXIS	United States Court of Appeals LEXIS cite
US Cl Ct LEXIS	United States Claims Court LEXIS cite
US Ct Cl LEXIS	United States Court of Claims LEXIS cite
US Claims LEXIS	United States Claims LEXIS cite
US Comp Gen LEXIS	United States Comptroller General LEXIS cite
US Dist LEXIS	United States District Court LEXIS cite
US LEXIS	United States Supreme Court LEXIS cite
US Tax Cas (CCH)	United States Tax Cases (CCH)
US Tax Ct LEXIS	United States Tax Court LEXIS cite
US Vet App LEXIS	United States Veteran's Appeals LEXIS cite
USCMA	United States Court of Military Appeals
USLW	United States Law Week (BNA)

USPQ (BNA)	United States Patents Quarterly (BNA)
USPQ 2d (BNA)	United States Patents Quarterly 2d (BNA)
UCLA Envtl L & Pol'y	UCLA Environmental Law & Policy
UCLA L Rev	UCLA Law Review
UCLA PAC BASIN LJ	UCLA Pacific Basin Law Journal
UCLA Women's LJ	UCLA Women's Law Journal
UMKC L Rev	University of Missouri at Kansas City Law Review
Ut ALS	Utah Advance Legislative Service
Ut Ch	Utah Chapter
Ut HB	Utah House Bill
Ut Resolution	Utah Resolution
Ut SB	Utah Senate Bill
Utah	Utah Reports
Utah 2d	Utah Reports 2d series
Utah Adv Rep	Utah Advance Reports
Utah AG LEXIS	Utah Attorney General LEXIS cite
Utah App LEXIS	Utah Court of Appeals LEXIS cite
Utah L Rev	Utah Law Review
Utah Laws	Utah Laws
Utah LEXIS	Utah Supreme Court LEXIS cite
Utah Sec LEXIS	Utah Securities Commission LEXIS cite
Utah Sec No-Act LEXIS	Utah SLC No-Action LEXIS cite
Utah Tax LEXIS	Utah State Tax Commission LEXIS cite

V

VI Act	Virgin Islands Act
VI ALS	Virgin Islands Advance Legislative Service
VI Bill	Virgin Islands Bill
VI LEXIS	Virgin Islands LEXIS cite
VI Resolution	Virgin Islands Resolution
VI SESS LAWS	Virgin Islands Session Laws

VA BCA LEXIS	Veterans Administration Board of Contract Appeals LEXIS cite
Va	Virginia Reports
Va Acts	Virginia Acts
Va AG LEXIS	Virginia Attorney General LEXIS cite
Va ALS	Virginia Advance Legislative Service
Va App	Virginia Court of Appeals Reports
Va App LEXIS	Virginia Court of Appeals LEXIS cite
Va Ch	Virginia Chapter
Va Envtl LJ	Virginia Environmental Law Journal
Va HB	Virginia House Bill
Va HJR	Virginia House Joint Resolution
Va J Int'l L	Virginia Journal of International Law
Va L Rev	Virginia Law Review
Va LEXIS	Virginia Supreme Court LEXIS cite
Va SB	Virginia Senate Bill
Va Sec LEXIS	Virginia Securities Commission LEXIS cite
Va SJR	Virginia Senate Joint Resolution
Va Tax LEXIS	Virginia Department of Taxation LEXIS cite
Va Tax Rev	Virginia Tax Review
Val Rep	Interstate Commerce Commission Valuation Reports
Val UL Rev	Valparaiso University Law Review
Vand L	Vanderbilt Law Review
Vet App	Veteran's Appeals
Vill Envtl LJ	Villanova Environmental Law Journal
Vill L Rev	Villanova Law Review
VLR	Virginia Law Reporter
Vt Laws	Vermont Laws
Vt	Vermont Reports
Vt ACT	Vermont Act
Vt ALS	Vermont Advance Legislative Service

Vt H	Vermont House
Vt LEXIS	Vermont Supreme Court LEXIS cite
Vt S	Vermont Senate
Vt Tax LEXIS	Vermont Department of Taxation LEXIS cite

W

W Va	West Virginia Reports
W Va Acts	West Virginia Acts
W Va AG LEXIS	West Virginia Attorney General LEXIS cite
W Va LEXIS	West Virginia Supreme Court LEXIS cite
W Va Tax LEXIS	West Virginia Tax LEXIS cite
WV ALS	West Virginia Advance Legislative Service
WV Ch	West Virginia Chapter
WV HB	West Virginia House Bill
WV HJR	West Virginia House Joint Resolution
WV SB	West Virginia Senate Bill
WV HR	West Virginia House Resolution
WV SJR	West Virginia Senate Joint Resolution
WV SR	West Virginia Senate Resolution
Wa Ch Laws	Washington Chapter Laws
Wa HJR	Washington House Joint Resolution
Wa ALS	Washington Advance Legislative Service
Wa Ch	Washington Chapter
Wa HB	Washington House Bill
Wa Init	Washington Initiative
Wa SB	Washington Senate Bill
Wa Sec LEXIS	Washington Securities Commission LEXIS cite
Wage & Hour Cas (BNA)	Wage & Hour Cases (BNA)
Wage & Hour Cas 2d (BNA)	Wage & Hour Cases 2d series (BNA)
Wake Forest L Rev	Wake Forest Law Review

Wall	Wallace's Reports (United States)
Wall J	J.W. Wallace's United States Circuit Court
Ware	Ware's United States District Court Reports
Wash & Lee L Rev	Washington & Lee Law Review
Wash	Washington Reports
Wash 2d	Washington Reports 2d series
Wash AG LEXIS	Washington Attorney General LEXIS cite
Wash App	Washington Appellate Reports
Wash App LEXIS	Washington Court of Appeals LEXIS cite
Wash L Rev	Washington Law Review
Wash LEXIS	Washington Supreme Court LEXIS cite
Wash Tax LEXIS	Washington Board of Tax Appeals LEXIS cite
Wash ULQ	Washington University Law Quarterly
Wash UTC LEXIS	Washington Utilities & Transportation Commission LEXIS cite
Weekly L Bull	Weekly Law Bulletin
West Law J	Western Law Journal
Wheeler Cr	Wheeler's Criminal Cases
Whittier L Rev	Whittier Law Review
Wis	Wisconsin Reports
Wis 2d	Wisconsin Reports 2d series
Wis AB	Wisconsin Assembly Bill
Wis Act	Wisconsin Act
Wis ALS	Wisconsin Advance Legislative Service
Wis AJR	Wisconsin Assembly Joint Resolution
Wis Joint Res	Wisconsin Joint Resolution
Wis SJR	Wisconsin Senate Joint Resolution
Wis L Rev	Wisconsin Law Review
Wis Laws	Wisconsin Laws
Wis SB	Wisconsin Senate Bill
Wisc AG LEXIS	Wisconsin Attorney General LEXIS cite
Wis App	Wisconsin Court of Appeals Reports

Wisc App LEXIS	Wisconsin Court of Appeals LEXIS cite
Wisc LEXIS	Wisconsin Supreme Court LEXIS cite
Wisc PUC LEXIS	Wisconsin Public Utilities Wisc Sec LEXIS
Wisc Tax LEXIS	Wisconsin Tax Appeals Commission LEXIS cite
Wm and Mary L Rev	William & Mary Law Review
Wm & Mary Bill of Rts J	William & Mary Bill of Rights Journal
Wm & Mary Rev Va L	William & Mary Review of Virginia Law
WmMitchell L Rev	William Mitchell Law Review
Woods	Woods United States Circuit Court Reports
Wool	Woolworth's Circuit Court Reports
Wy ALS	Wyoming Advance Legislative Service
Wy Ch	Wyoming Chapter
Wy EA	Wyoming Enrolled Act
Wy HF	Wyoming House File
Wy HB	Wyoming House Bill
Wy No-Act LEXIS	Wyoming No-Action LEXIS cite
Wy SB	Wyoming Senate Bill
Wy Sec LEXIS	Wyoming Securities Commission LEXIS cite
Wy SF	Wyoming Senate File
Wyo	Wyoming Reports
Wyo AG LEXIS	Wyoming Attorney General LEXIS cite
Wyo LEXIS	Wyoming Supreme Court LEXIS cite
Wyo Sess Laws	Wyoming Session Laws
Wyo Tax LEXIS	Wyoming Tax Commission LEXIS cite

XYZ

Yale J on Reg	Yale Journal on Regulations
Yale LJ	Yale Law Journal

LEXSTAT Citation Formats

STATE	CITATION FORMAT
Alabama (AL) Code of Alabama (Michie)	al code x
Alaska (AK) Alaska Statutes (Michie)	ak code x
Arizona (AZ) Arizona Revised Statutes	az code x
Arkansas (AR) Arkansas Statutes Annotated (Michie)	ar code x

California (CA)
   Deering's California Codes Annotated
     (LCP)
	ca (CODE TOPIC) code x
	     Example: ca civil code 1365

CODE TOPICS AVAILABLE IN CALIFORNIA STATUTES

Bus. & Prof.	Evidence	Health & Saf.	Pub. Cont.	Uncod. Wate.
Civil	Finance	Insurance	Pub. Res.	Uncod. Init.
Civil Proc.	Fish & Game	Labor	Pub. Util.	Unemp. Ins.
Corporations	Food & Agric.	Mil. & Vet.	Rev. & Tax.	Vehicle
Education	Government	Penal	Sts. & High.	Water
Election	Harb. & Nav.	Probate	U.C.C.	Welf. & Inst.

Barclays Official California Code of Regulations	x ca admin x

(continued)

STATE	CITATION FORMAT
Colorado (CO)	
Colorado Revised Statutes	co code x
Connecticut (CT)	
General Statutes of Connecticut	ct code x
Delaware (DE)	
Michie's Delaware Revised Code	x de code x
District of Columbia (DC)	
District of Columbia Code Annotated (Michie)	dc code x
Florida (FL)	
Florida Statutes	fl code x
Florida Administrative Code	fl admin x
Georgia (GA)	
Georgia Code Annotated (Michie)	ga code x
Hawaii (HI)	
Hawaii Revised Statutes	hi code x
Idaho (ID)	
Idaho Code (Michie)	id code x
Illinois (IL)	
*Illinois Revised Statutes	il code x
Indiana (IN)	
Michie's Burns Indiana Statutes Annotated	in code x
Iowa (IA)	
Code of Iowa	ia code x
Kansas (KS)	
Kansas Statutes Annotated	ks code x
Kansas Administrative Regulations	ks admin x
Kentucky (KY)	
Banks-Baldwin's Kentucky Revised Statutes Annotated	ky code x baldwin

Kentucky Revised Statutes Annotated
    (Michie)

ky code x michie

Louisiana (LA)
    *Louisiana Revised Statutes

la (CODE TOPIC) x
    Example: la cjp 2

CODE TOPICS AVAILABLE IN LOUISIANA

Juvenile Procedure = cjp	Criminal Procedure = ccrp
Civil Procedure = ccp	Revised Statutes = rev stat
Civil Code = cc	

Maine (ME)
    *Maine Revised Statutes

x me code x

Maryland (MD)
    Annotated Code of Maryland (Michie)
    (Maryland sections can be cited
        using a code topic or
        article & section number.)

md (CODE TOPIC) code
md code art x @ x
    Examples: md real prop 1-101
    md code art 1 @ 1

CODE TOPICS AVAILABLE IN MARYLAND

Agriculture	Est. & Trusts	Real Prop.
Bus. Occ. & Prof.	Family Law	State Fin. & Proc.
Commercial Law	Fin. Inst.	State Gov't
Corp. & Ass'ns	Health-Gen.	Tax-Gen.
Cts. & Jud. Proc.	Health-Occ.	Tax-Prop.
Education	Labor & Employ.	Transportation
Environment	Nat. Res.	

Massachusetts (MA)
    Annotated Laws of Massachusetts

ma code ch x @ x

Michigan (MI)
    Michigan Compiled Laws

mi code x

Minnesota (MN)
    Minnesota Statutes
    Minnesota Rules (Administrative Code)

mn code x
mn admin x

(*continued*)

STATE	CITATION FORMAT
Mississippi (MS)	
Mississippi Code Annotated	ms code x
Missouri (MO)	
Revised Statutes of Missouri	mo code x
Montana (MT)	
Montana Code Annotated	mt code x
Nebraska (NE)	
Revised Statutes of Nebraska	ne code x
Nevada (NV)	
Nevada Revised Statutes Annotated (Michie)	nv code x
New Hampshire (NH)	
New Hampshire Revised Statutes Annotated	nh code x
New Jersey (NJ)	
*New Jersey Revised Statutes	nj code x
New Mexico (NM)	
New Mexico Statutes Annotated (Michie)	nm code x
New York (NY)	
New York Consolidated Laws Service	ny (CODE TOPIC) code x Example: ny dom rel code 7

CODE TOPICS AVAILABLE IN NEW YORK

Aband. Prop.	Civ. Prac. Laws & Rules	Dom. Relations
Agric. Conserv. & Adj.	Civ. Rights	Education
Agric. & Markets	Civ. Service	Election
Alco. Bev. Control	Commerce	Em. Domain Proc.
Arts & Cult. Affairs	Coop. Corp.	Employer's Liab.
Banking	Correction	Energy
Benev. Orders	County	Envir. Conserv.
Bus. Corp.	Crim. Procedure	Est. Powers & Trust
Canal	Debt. & Credit	Executive

CODE TOPICS AVAILABLE IN NEW YORK

Fam. Ct. Act	Insurance	Mult. Residence
Gen. Ass'ns	Judiciary	Mun. Home Rule
Gen. Business	Labor	Navigation
Gen. City	Legislative	Not-for-Profit Corp.
Gen. Constr.	Lien	Opt. County Gov't
Gen. Mun.	Local Finance	Parks, Rec. & Hist. Pres.
Gen. Oblig.	Mental Hygiene	Partnership
Highway	Military	Penal
Indian	Mult. Dwelling	Personal Prop.
Priv. Hous. Fin.	Railroad	Rural Elec. Coop.
Pub. Authorities	Rapid Transit	Second Class Cities
Pub. Buildings	Real Prop.	Social Services
Pub. Health	Real Prop. Acts	Soil & Water Conserv. Dist.
Pub. Housing	Real Prop. Tax	State
Pub. Lands	Relig. Corp.	State A.P.A.
Pub. Officers	Retire. & Soc. Sec.	State Finance
Pub. Service	Town	Unconsolidated
Racing, Pari-Mut.	Transportation	Veh. & Traffic
Wag. & Breeding	Transp. Corp.	Village
Surrogate's Ct.	U.C.C.	Vol. Ambulance Worker's Ben.
Proc. Act	State Print. & Pub. Docs.	Vol. Firefighter's Ben.
Tax	Statute of Local Gov'ts	Worker's Comp.

STATE	CITATION FORMAT
North Carolina (NC)	
Michie's General Statutes of North Carolina	nc code x
North Dakota (ND)	
North Dakota Century Code (Michie)	nd code x

(continued)

STATE	CITATION FORMAT
Ohio (OH)	
Banks–Baldwin's Ohio Revised Code Annotated	oh code x
Ohio Administrative Code (Banks–Baldwin)	oh admin x
Oklahoma (OK)	
*Oklahoma Statutes	x ok code x
Oregon (OR)	
Oregon Revised Statutes	or code x
Pennsylvania (PA)	
*Pennsylvania Statutes	x pa code x
Pennsylvania Administrative Code	x pa admin x

The statutes of the state of Pennsylvania have been added to LEXIS by MDC and are being made available under license from West Publishing Company and George T. Bisel Company.

Puerto Rico (PR)	
Laws of Puerto Rico Annotated	x pr code x
Rhode Island (RI)	
General Laws of Rhode Island (Michie)	ri code x
South Carolina (SC)	
Code of Laws of South Carolina	sc code x
South Dakota (SD)	
South Dakota Codified Laws Annotated (Michie)	sd code x
Tennessee (TN)	
Tennessee Code Annotated (Michie)	tn code x
Texas (TX)	
*Texas Statutes and Codes	tx (CODE TOPIC) code x tx (CODE TOPIC) code art x Example: tx penal code 1.01

CODE TOPICS AVAILABLE IN TEXAS

Agriculture	Education	Insurance	Property
Alco. Beverage	Election	Local Gov't	Rev. Civ. Stat.
Bus. & Commerce	Family	Natural Res.	Tax
Bus. Corp. Act.	Government	Parks & Wild.	Water
Civ. Prac. & Rem-	Health & Safety	Penal	
Code Crim. Proc.	Human Res.	Probate	

The statutes of the state of Texas have been added to LEXIS by MDC and are being made available under license from West Publishing Company.

Utah (UT)
    Utah Code Annotated (Michie)   ut code x

Vermont (VT)
    Vermont Statutes Annotated   x vt code x

Virgin Islands (VI)
    Virgin Islands Code Annotated   x vi code x

Virginia (VA)
    Code of Virginia (Michie)   va code x

Washington (WA)
    Revised Code of Washington   wa code x

West Virginia (WV)
    West Virginia Code (Michie)   wv code x

Wisconsin (WI)
    Wisconsin Statutes   wi code x

Wyoming (WY)
    Wyoming Statutes Annotated (Michie)   wy code x

Federal Materials

PUBLICATION	CITATION FORMAT
United States Code Service (US)	x uscs x
Internal Revenue Code (IRC)	irc x
Code of Federal Regulations (CFR)	x cfr x
Federal Sentencing Guidelines (USSG)	ussg x
Witkin Summary of California Law	ws (chapter) x
(WITSUM)	Example: ws contracts 11

CHAPTERS AVAILABLE IN WITKIN SUMMARY OF CALIF. LAW

Agency	Equity	Pers Prop	Tax
Com Prop	H&W	Real Prop	Torts
Const Law	Neg Inst	Sales	Trusts
Contracts	P&C	Sec Trans-Pers P	Wills
Corp	Partn	Sec Trans-Real P	Work Comp

Official text and comments of the Uniform	ucc x-x
Commercial Code (UCC)	Example: ucc 4-102

LEXIS Cites in Auto-Cite

TITLE, FORUM, OR JURISDICTION	CITATION FORMAT
ALABAMA COURT OF CIVIL APPEALS	ALA CIV APP LEXIS
ALABAMA COURT OF CRIMINAL APPEALS	ALA CRIM APP LEXIS
ALABAMA SUPREME COURT	ALA LEXIS
ALASKA COURT OF APPEALS	ALAS APP LEXIS
ALASKA SUPREME COURT	ALAS LEXIS
ARIZONA COURT OF APPEALS	ARIZ APP LEXIS

TITLE, FORUM, OR JURISDICTION	CITATION FORMAT
ARIZONA SUPREME COURT	ARIZ LEXIS
ARKANSAS COURT OF APPEALS	ARK APP LEXIS
ARKANSAS SUPREME COURT	ARK LEXIS
BANKRUPTCY COURT, U.S.	BANKR LEXIS
CALIFORNIA COURT OF APPEALS	CAL APP LEXIS
CALIFORNIA SUPREME COURT	CAL LEXIS
CLAIMS COURT, U.S.	US CL CT LEXIS
COLORADO COURT OF APPEALS	COLO APP LEXIS
COLORADO SUPREME COURT	COLO LEXIS
COMMON PLEAS COURT OF PHILADELPHIA COUNTY	PHIL CTY RPTR LEXIS
CONNECTICUT APPELLATE COURT	CONN APP LEXIS
CONNECTICUT CIRCUIT COURT	CONN CIR LEXIS
CONNECTICUT SUPERIOR COURT & COURT OF COMMON PLEAS	CONN SUPER LEXIS
CONNECTICUT SUPREME COURT	CONN LEXIS
COURT OF APPEALS, U.S.	US APP LEXIS
COURT OF INTERNATIONAL TRADE, U.S.	CT INTL TRADE LEXIS
COURT OF MILITARY APPEALS, U.S.	CMA LEXIS
COURT OF MILITARY REVIEW, U.S.	CMR LEXIS
COURT OF VETERANS APPEALS, U.S.	US VET APP LEXIS
DELAWARE COURT OF CHANCERY	DEL CH LEXIS
DELAWARE DEPT. OF FINANCE, DIVISION OF REVENUE	DEL TAX LEXIS
DELAWARE SUPERIOR COURT	DEL SUPER LEXIS
DELAWARE SUPREME COURT	DEL LEXIS

(*continued*)

TITLE, FORUM, OR JURISDICTION	CITATION FORMAT
DISTRICT COURT, U.S.	US DIST LEXIS
DISTRICT OF COLUMBIA APPEALS COURT	DC APP LEXIS
FLORIDA DISTRICT COURTS OF APPEAL	FLA APP LEXIS
FLORIDA SUPREME COURT	FLA LEXIS
GEORGIA COURT OF APPEALS	GA APP LEXIS
GEORGIA SUPREME COURT	GA LEXIS
HAWAII INTERMEDIATE COURT OF APPEALS	HAW APP LEXIS
HAWAII SUPREME COURT	HAW LEXIS
IDAHO COURT OF APPEALS	IDA APP LEXIS
IDAHO SUPREME COURT	IDA LEXIS
ILLINOIS APPELLATE COURT	ILL APP LEXIS
ILLINOIS SUPREME COURT	ILL LEXIS
INDIANA APPEALS COURT	IND APP LEXIS
INDIANA SUPREME COURT	IND LEXIS
IOWA APPEALS COURT	IOWA APP LEXIS
IOWA SUPREME COURT	IOWA LEXIS
KANSAS COURT OF APPEALS	KAN APP LEXIS
KANSAS SUPREME COURT	KAN LEXIS
KENTUCKY COURT OF APPEALS	KY APP LEXIS
KENTUCKY SUPREME COURT	KY LEXIS
LOUISIANA BOARD OF TAX APPEALS	LA TAX LEXIS
LOUISIANA COURTS OF APPEALS	LA APP LEXIS
LOUISIANA SUPREME COURT	LA LEXIS
MAINE SUPREME COURT	ME LEXIS
MARYLAND COURT OF APPEALS	MD LEXIS

TITLE, FORUM, OR JURISDICTION	CITATION FORMAT
MARYLAND COURT OF SPECIAL APPEALS	MD APP LEXIS
MASSACHUSETTS APPEALS COURT	MASS APP LEXIS
MASSACHUSETTS SUPREME JUDICIAL COURT	MASS LEXIS
MICHIGAN COURT OF APPEALS	MICH APP LEXIS
MICHIGAN SUPREME COURT	MICH LEXIS
MINNESOTA APPEALS COURT	MINN APP LEXIS
MINNESOTA SUPREME COURT	MINN LEXIS
MISSISSIPPI SUPREME COURT	MISS LEXIS
MISSOURI COURT OF APPEALS	MO APP LEXIS
MISSOURI SUPREME COURT	MO LEXIS
MONTANA SUPREME COURT	MONT LEXIS
NEBRASKA SUPREME COURT	NEB LEXIS
NEVADA SUPREME COURT	NEV LEXIS
NEW HAMPSHIRE SUPREME COURT	NH LEXIS
NEW JERSEY SUPERIOR COURT	NJ SUPER LEXIS
NEW JERSEY SUPREME COURT	NJ LEXIS
NEW JERSEY TAX COURT	NJ TAX LEXIS
NEW MEXICO COURT OF APPEALS	NM APP LEXIS
NEW MEXICO SUPREME COURT	NM LEXIS
NEW YORK COURT OF APPEALS	NY APP LEXIS
NEW YORK SUPREME COURT	NY MISC LEXIS
NEW YORK SUPREME COURT, APPELLATE DIVISION	NY APP DIV LEXIS
NORTH CAROLINA COURT OF APPEALS	NC APP LEXIS
NORTH CAROLINA SUPREME COURT	NC LEXIS

(*continued*)

TITLE, FORUM, OR JURISDICTION	CITATION FORMAT
NORTH DAKOTA COURT OF APPEALS	ND APP LEXIS
NORTH DAKOTA SUPREME COURT	ND LEXIS
OCCUPATIONAL SAFETY & HEALTH REVIEW COMMISSION	OSAHRC LEXIS
OHIO COURTS OF APPEAL	OHIO APP LEXIS
OHIO MISCELLANEOUS COURTS	OHIO MISC LEXIS
OHIO SUPREME COURT	OHIO LEXIS
OKLAHOMA COURT OF APPEALS	OKLA CIV APP LEXIS
OKLAHOMA COURT OF CRIMINAL APPEALS	OKLA CRIM APP LEXIS
OKLAHOMA SUPREME COURT	OKLA LEXIS
OREGON COURT OF APPEALS	ORE APP LEXIS
OREGON SUPREME COURT	ORE LEXIS
OREGON TAX COURT	ORE TAX LEXIS
PENNSYLVANIA COMMONWEALTH COURT	PA COMMW LEXIS
PENNSYLVANIA COMMONWEALTH COURT DECISIONS APPEALED FROM BOARD OF FINANCE AND REVENUE	PA TAX LEXIS
PENNSYLVANIA SUPERIOR COURT	PA SUPER LEXIS
PENNSYLVANIA SUPREME COURT	PA LEXIS
RHODE ISLAND SUPREME COURT	RI LEXIS
SOUTH CAROLINA COURT OF APPEALS	SC APP LEXIS
SOUTH CAROLINA SUPREME COURT	SC LEXIS
SOUTH DAKOTA SUPREME COURT	SD LEXIS
SUPREME COURT, U.S.	US LEXIS
TAX COURT, U.S.	US TAX CT LEXIS
TAX COURT MEMORANDA, U.S.	TAX CT MEMO LEXIS

TITLE, FORUM, OR JURISDICTION	CITATION FORMAT
TENNESSEE COURT OF APPEALS	TENN APP LEXIS
TENNESSEE COURT OF CRIMINAL APPEALS	TENN CRIM APP LEXIS
TENNESSEE SUPREME COURT	TENN LEXIS
TEXAS COURT OF CRIMINAL APPEALS	TEX CRIM APP LEXIS
TEXAS COURTS OF APPEAL; TEXAS COURTS OF CIVIL APPEAL	TEX APP LEXIS
TEXAS SUPREME COURT	TEX LEXIS
UTAH COURT OF APPEALS	UTAH APP LEXIS
UTAH SUPREME COURT	UTAH LEXIS
VERMONT SUPREME COURT	VT LEXIS
VIRGINIA COURT OF APPEALS	VA APP LEXIS
VIRGINIA SUPREME COURT	VA LEXIS
WASHINGTON COURT OF APPEALS	WASH APP LEXIS
WASHINGTON SUPREME COURT	WASH LEXIS
WEST VIRGINIA SUPREME COURT	W VA LEXIS
WISCONSIN APPEALS COURT	WISC APP LEXIS
WISCONSIN SUPREME COURT	WISC LEXIS
WYOMING SUPREME COURT	WYO LEXIS

Auto-Cite Reporters

REPORTER	AUTO–CITE ABBREVIATION
ADDISON REPORTS (PA)	ADDISON
ADVANCE SHEETS (MA)	ADVSHEETS
AIKEN'S REPORTER (VT)	AIK
ALABAMA REPORTER	ALA
ALABAMA APPELLATE COURT REPORTS	ALAAPP
ALASKA REPORTS	ALASKA
AMERICAN FEDERAL TAX REPORTS	AFTR
AMERICAN LAW REPORTS ANNOTATED	ALR
AMERICAN LAW REPORTS, 2ND	ALR2D
AMERICAN LAW REPORTS, 3RD	ALR3D
AMERICAN LAW REPORTS, 4TH	ALR4TH
AMERICAN LAW REPORTS ANNOTATED FEDERAL	ALRFED
AMERICAN MARITIME CASES	AMC
APPELLATE DIVISION REPORTS (NY)	APPDIV (AD)
APPELLATE DIVISION REPORTS, 2ND (NY)	APPDIV2D (AD2D)
ARIZONA REPORTS	ARIZ
ARIZONA ADVANCE REPORTS	ARIZADVR
ARIZONA APPEALS REPORTS	ARIZAPP
ARKANSAS REPORTS	AR
ARKANSAS COURT OF APPEALS REPORTS	ARKAPP
ATLANTIC REPORTER	A
ATLANTIC REPORTER, 2ND	A2D
BREESE'S REPORTS, APPENDIX (IL)	BREESEAPPX
BRIEF TIMES REPORTER (CO)	BTR

(continued)

REPORTER	AUTO-CITE ABBREVIATION
BURNETT'S REPORTS (WI)	BURNETT
CALIFORNIA REPORTS	CAL (C)
CALIFORNIA REPORTS, 2ND	CAL2D (C2D)
CALIFORNIA REPORTS, 3RD	CAL3D (C3D)
CALIFORNIA APPELLATE REPORTS	CALAPP (CA)
CALIFORNIA APPELLATE REPORTS, 2ND	CALAPP2D (CA2D)
CALIFORNIA APPELLATE REPORTS, 3RD	CALAPP3D (CA3D)
CALIFORNIA REPORTER	CALRPTR
CALIFORNIA UNREPORTED CASES	CALUNREP
CALIFORNIA APP RPTS 1ST SERIES SUPP	CAS
CALIFORNIA APP RPTS 2ND SERIES SUPP	CA2DS
CALIFORNIA APP RPTS 3RD SERIES SUPP	CA3DS
CAROLINA LAW REPOSITORY (4 NC)	CARLREPOS
CCH BANKRUPTCY LAW REPORTER	CCHBLR
CCH EMPLOYMENT PRACTICES DECISIONS	CCHEPD
CCH FEDERAL SECURITIES LAW REPORTER	CCHFSLR
CCH LABOR CASES	CCHLC
CCH NATIONAL LABOR RELATIONS BOARD DEC.	CCHNLRB
CCH OCCUPATIONAL SAFETY & HEALTH DECISIONS	CCHOSHD
CCH PRODUCTS LIABILITY REPORTS	CCHPLR
CCH TRADE CASES	CCHTC
CCH UNEMPLOYMENT INSURANCE REPORT	CCHUIR
CHANDLER'S REPORTS (WI)	CHAND
COLLIER'S BANKRUPTCY CASES	CBC
COLLIER'S BANKRUPTCY CASES, 2ND	CBC2D
COLORADO REPORTS	COLO
COLORADO APPEALS REPORTS	COLOAPP
COURT OF APPEALS FOR FEDERAL CIRCUIT	FEDCIR
CUMULATIVE BULLETIN (IRS)	CB

REPORTER	AUTO-CITE ABBREVIATION
CUSTOMS APPEALS DECISIONS (BY NUMBER)	CAD
CONNECTICUT REPORTS	CONN
CONNECTICUT APPELLATE COURTS	CONNAPP
CONNECTICUT CIRCUIT REPORTS	CONNCIR
CONNECTICUT SUPPLEMENT	CONNSUP
CONTRACT CASES FEDERAL	CCF
DAKOTA REPORTS (ND, SD)	DAK
DAY'S REPORTS (CT)	DAY
D. CHIPMAN'S REPORTS (VT)	DCHIP
DELAWARE REPORTS	DEL
DELAWARE CHANCERY REPORTS	DELCH
DISTRICT OF COLUMBIA REPORTS	DISTCOL
DOUGLAS REPORTS (MI)	DOUGL
DUDLEY'S GEORGIA REPORTS	DUDLEY
EMPLOYEE BENEFITS CASES (BNA)	EBC
ENVIRONMENTAL LAW REPORTER	ELR
FAIR EMPLOYMENT PRACTICES (BNA)	FEP
FEDERAL REPORTER	F
FEDERAL REPORTER, 2ND	F2D
FEDERAL RULES DECISIONS	FRD
FEDERAL RULES OF EVIDENCE SERVICE	FRESERV
FEDERAL RULES OF EVIDENCE SERVICE, 2ND	FRSERV2D
FEDERAL RULES OF EVIDENCE SERVICE, 3RD	FRSERV3D
FEDERAL SUPPLEMENT	FSUPP
FLORIDA REPORTS (OFFICIAL)	FLA
FLORIDA SUPPLEMENT	FLASUPP
FLORIDA SUPPLEMENT, 2ND	FLASUPP2D
FLORIDA LAW WEEKLY	FLW
FREEMAN'S MISSISSIPPI CHANCERY REPORTS	FREEMCH
GEORGIA REPORTS	GA

(continued)

REPORTER	AUTO-CITE ABBREVIATION
GEORGIA APPEALS REPORTS	GAAPP
GEORGIA DECISIONS PART 1	GADECPT1
GEORGIA DECISIONS PART 2	GADECPT2
GEORGE GREENE'S IOWA REPORTS	GGREENE
GILL'S REPORTS (MD)	GILL
GILL & JOHNSON'S MARYLAND REPORTS	GILL&J
GRANT'S PENNSYLVANIA CASES	GRANTCAS
HARRINGTON'S MICHIGAN CHANCERY REPORTS	HARRCH
HARRIS & GILL'S REPORTS (MD)	HARR&G
HARRIS & JOHNSON'S REPORTS (MD)	HARR&J
HARRIS & MCHENRY (MD)	HARR&MCH
HAWAII REPORTS	HAWAII
HAWAII APPELLATE REPORTS	HAWAPP
HAYWOOD'S NC REPORTS (2-3 NC)	HAYW
HOUSTON'S CRIMINAL CASES (DE)	HOUSTCRIM
HOWELL, NISI PRIUS (MI)	HOWNP
HUN NEW YORK SUPREME COURT REPORTS	HUN
IDAHO REPORTS	IDAHO
ILLINOIS REPORTS	ILL
ILLINOIS REPORTS, 2ND	ILL2D
ILLINOIS APPELLATE COURT REPORTS	ILLAPP
ILLINOIS APPELLATE COURT REPORTS (ABSTRACTS)	ILLAPP(A)
ILLINOIS APPELLATE COURT REPORTS, 2ND	ILLAPP2D
ILLINOIS APPELLATE COURT REPORTS, 2ND (ABSTRACTS)	ILLA2D(A)
ILLINOIS APPELLATE COURT REPORTS, 3RD	ILLAPP3D
ILLINOIS APPELLATE COURT REPORTS, 3RD (ABSTRACTS)	ILLAPP3D(A)
ILLINOIS CIRCUIT COURT REPORTS	ILLCC
ILLINOIS DECISIONS	ILLDEC

REPORTER	AUTO-CITE ABBREVIATION
IMMIGRATION & NATIONALITY LAWS OF U.S. (ADMINISTRATIVE DECISIONS UNDER)	I&NDEC
IMMIGRATION NATURALIZATION INTERIM DEC	INTDECNO
INDIANA REPORTS	IND
INDIANA APPELLATE COURT REPORTS	INDAPP
INDIAN TERRITORY REPORTS	INDIANTERR
INTERNAL REVENUE BULLETIN	IRB
INDIVIDUAL EMPLOYMENT RIGHTS CASES (BNA)	IER
IOWA REPORTS	IOWA
JEFFERSON'S REPORTS (VA)	JEFF
KANSAS REPORTS	KAN
KANSAS APPEALS REPORTS	KANAPP
KANSAS APPEALS REPORTS, 2ND	KANAPP2D
KENTUCKY REPORTS	KY
KENTUCKY LAW REPORTER	KYLR
KENTUCKY LAW REPORTER, ABSTRACTS	KYLR(ABS)
KENTUCKY COURT OF APPEALS OPINIONS	KYOPS
KIRBY'S REPORTS & SUPPLEMENT (CT)	KIRBY
LABOR RELATIONS REFERENCE MANUAL (BNA)	LRRM
LESTER'S SUPP TO 33 GA	GASUPP
LOS ANGELES DAILY JOURNAL	DAR
LOUISIANA REPORTS	LA
LOUISIANA ANNUAL REPORTS	LAANN
LOUISIANA COURT OF APPEALS REPORTS	LAAPP
LOUISIANA COURT OF APPEALS, PARISH OF ORLEANS	ORLEANSAPP
MACARTHUR'S REPORTS (8-10 DIST COL)	MACARTH
MACARTHUR'S & MACKEY'S RPTS (11 DIST COL)	MACARTH&M
MACKEY'S REPORTS (12-20 DIST COL)	MACKEY
MAINE REPORTS	ME
MANNING'S UNREPORTED CASES (LA)	MANUNREP

(*continued*)

REPORTER	AUTO-CITE ABBREVIATION
MARTIN'S REPORTS (LA)	MART
MARTIN'S NC REPORTS (1 NC)	MARTIN
MARTIN'S LOUISIANA REPORTS, NEW SERIES	MARTNS
MARYLAND REPORTS	MD
MARYLAND APPELLATE REPORTS	MDAPP
MARYLAND CHANCERY REPORTS	MDCH
MASSACHUSETTS REPORTS	MASS
MASSACHUSETTS APPELLATE DIVISION	MASSAD
MASSACHUSETTS APPELLATE REPORTS	MASSAPP
MASSACHUSETTS APPELLATE DECISIONS	MASSAPPDEC
MCCAHON'S KANSAS REPORTS	MCCAHON
MCGLOIN'S COURT OF APPEALS REPORTS (LA)	MCGLOIN
MEDIA LAW REPORTER (BNA)	MEDIALR
MICHIGAN REPORTS	MICH
MICHIGAN COURT OF APPEALS REPORTS	MICHAPP
MICHIGAN NISI PRIUS CASES	MICHNP
MINNESOTA REPORTS	MINN
MINNOR'S REPORTS (AL)	MINOR
MISCELLANEOUS REPORTS (NY)	MISC
MISCELLANEOUS REPORTS, 2ND (NY)	MISC2D
MISSISSIPPI REPORTS	MISS
MILITARY JUSTICE	MJ
MISSOURI REPORTS	MO
MISSOURI APPEALS REPORTS	MOAPP
MONAGHAN'S REPORTS (PA)	MONAGHAN
MONTANA REPORTS	MONT
MORRIS' REPORTS (IA)	MORRIS
NATIONAL LABOR RELATIONS BOARD (DECISIONS & ORDERS OF)	NLRB
NATIONAL LABOR RELATIONS BOARD (DECISIONS & ORDERS OF—BY CASE NUMBER)	NLRBNO

REPORTER	AUTO-CITE ABBREVIATION
N. CHIPMAN'S REPORTS (VT)	NCHIP
NEBRASKA REPORTS	NEB
NEBRASKA UNOFFICIAL REPORTS	NEBUNOF
NEVADA REPORTS	NEV
NEW HAMPSHIRE REPORTS	NH
NEW JERSEY REPORTS	NJ
NEW JERSEY EQUITY REPORTS	NJEQ
NEW JERSEY LAW REPORTS	NJL
NEW JERSEY MISCELLANEOUS REPORTS	NJMISC
NEW JERSEY SUPERIOR COURT REPORTS	NJSUPER
NEW JERSEY TAX COURT REPORTS	NJTAX
NEW MEXICO REPORTS	NM
NEW YORK REPORTS	NY
NEW YORK REPORTS, 2ND	NY2D
NEW YORK SUPPLEMENT REPORTS	NYS
NEW YORK SUPPLEMENT REPORTS, 2ND	NYS2D
NORTH CAROLINA REPORTS	NC
NORTH CAROLINA APPEALS REPORTS	NCAPP
NORTH CAROLINA TERM REPORTS (4 NC)	NCTERMREP
NORTH DAKOTA REPORTS	ND
NORTH EASTERN REPORTER	NE
NORTH EASTERN REPORTER, 2ND	NE2D
NORTH WESTERN REPORTER	NW
NORTH WESTERN REPORTER, 2ND	NW2D
OCCUPATIONAL SAFETY & HEALTH REPORTER (BNA)	OSHC
OHIO REPORTS	OHIO (O)
OHIO APPEALS REPORTS	OHIOAPP (OAPP)
OHIO APPEALS REPORTS, 2ND	OHIOAPP2D (OAPP2D)

(*continued*)

REPORTER	AUTO-CITE ABBREVIATION
OHIO APPEALS REPORTS, 3RD	OHIOAPP3D (OAPP3D)
OHIO STATE BAR ASSOCIATION REPORT	OHIOBR (OBR)
OHIO LAW ABSTRACT	OHIOLABS
OHIO MISCELLANEOUS REPORTS	OHIOMISC (OMISC)
OHIO MISCELLANEOUS REPORTS, 2ND	OMISC2D
OHIO OPINIONS	OHIOOPS (OOPS)
OHIO OPINIONS, 2ND	OHIOOPS2D (OOPS2D)
OHIO OPINIONS, 3RD	OHIOOPS3D (OOPS3D)
OHIO STATE REPORTS	OHIOST (OS)
OHIO STATE REPORTS, 2ND	OHIOST2D (OS2D)
OHIO STATE REPORTS, 3RD	OHIOST3D (OS3D)
OIL & GAS REPORTER	OGR
OKLAHOMA REPORTS	OKLA
OKLAHOMA CRIMINAL REPORTS	OKLACRIM
OREGON REPORTS	OR
OREGON APPEALS REPORTS	ORAPP
OREGON TAX REPORTS	OTR
PACIFIC REPORTER	P
PACIFIC REPORTER, 2ND	P2D
PATTON JR. & HEATH'S REPORTS (VA)	PATTON&H
PENNSYLVANIA REPORTS	PA
PENNSYLVANIA COMMONWEALTH REPORTS	PACMWLTH
PENNSYLVANIA DISTRICT & COUNTY REPORTS	PAD&C

REPORTER	AUTO-CITE ABBREVIATION
PENNSYLVANIA DISTRICT & COUNTY REPORTS, 2ND	PAD&C2D
PENNSYLVANIA DISTRICT & COUNTY REPORTS, 3RD	PAD&C3D
PENNSYLVANIA DISTRICT & COUNTY REPORTS, 4TH	PAD&C4TH
PENNSYLVANIA SUPERIOR COURT REPORTS	PASUPER
PENNYPACKER UNREPORTED PENN. CASES	PENNYP
PENROSE & WATTS REPORTS (PA)	PENR&W
PENDING OPINION REPORTS (OH)	POR
PINNEY'S REPORTS (WI)	PINNEY
PORTER'S REPORTS (AL)	PORT
POSEY UNREPORTED CASES (TX)	POSEYUNREP
QUINCY SUPERIOR COURT OF JUDICATURE (MA)	QUINCY
RAWLE'S REPORTS (PA)	RAWLE
RECORDER	CDOS
REVENUE PROCEDURES (IRS)	REVPROC
REVENUE RULINGS (IRS)	REVRUL
RHODE ISLAND REPORTER	RI
R.M. CHARLTON'S REPORTS (GA)	RMCHARLT
ROBINSON'S REPORTS (LA)	ROB
ROOT'S REPORTS (CT)	ROOT
SADLER'S CASES	SADLER
SAN FRANCISCO DAILY JOURNAL	DAR
SOUTH CAROLINA REPORTS	SC
SOUTH CAROLINA EQUITY REPORTS	SCEQ
SOUTH CAROLINA LAW REPORTS	SCL
SOUTH DAKOTA REPORTS	SD
SOUTH EASTERN REPORTER	SE
SOUTH EASTERN REPORTER, 2ND	SE2D
SERGEANT & RAWLE'S REPORTS (PA)	SERG&R

(*continued*)

REPORTER	AUTO-CITE ABBREVIATION
SHANNON'S UNREPORTED TENNESSEE CASES	SHANNONCAS
SMEDES & MARSHALL'S MISSISSIPPI CHANCERY	SMEDES&MCH
SMITH'S REPORTS (IN)	SMITH(IND)
SOUTHERN REPORTER	SO
SOUTHERN REPORTER, 2ND	SO2D
SOUTH WESTERN REPORTER	SW
SOUTH WESTERN REPORTER, 2ND	SW2D
STEWART'S REPORTS (AL)	STEW
STEWART & PORTER'S REPORTER (AL)	STEW&P
TAX COURT OF UNITED STATES	TC
TAX COURT OF UNITED STATES (BY NUMBER)	TCNO
TAYLOR'S REPORTS (1 NC)	TAYLOR
TENNESSEE REPORTS	TENN
TENNESSEE APPEALS REPORTS	TENNAPP
TENNESSEE COURT OF CIVIL APPEALS	TENNCCA
TENNESSEE CHANCERY REPORTS	TENNCH
TENNESSEE CHANCERY APPEALS	TENNCHAPP
TENNESSEE CRIMINAL COURT	TENNCRIM
TEXAS REPORTS	TEX
TEXAS APPEALS REPORTS	TEXAPP
TEXAS BANKRUPTCY COURT REPORTER	TEXBCR
TEXAS CIVIL APPEAL CASES	TEXAPPCIV
TEXAS CIVIL APPEALS	TEXCIVAPP
TEXAS CRIMINAL REPORTS	TEXCRIM
TEXAS SUPREME COURT JOURNAL	TEXSUPCJ
THACHER CRIMINAL CASES (MA)	THACHERCRIM
THOMPSON'S UNREPORTED TENNESSEE CASES	THOMPTENN
TREASURY DECISIONS (BY NUMBER)	TD
T.U.P. CHARLTON'S REPORTS (GA)	TUPCHARLT
TYLER'S REPORTS (VT)	TYLER

REPORTER	AUTO-CITE ABBREVIATION
UNIFORM COMMERCIAL CODE REPORTING SERVICE	UCCRS
UNIFORM COMMERCIAL CODE REPORTING SERVICE, 2ND	UCCRS2D
UNITED STATES LAW WEEK	USLW
UNITED STATES PATENTS QUARTERLY	USPQ
UNITED STATES PATENTS QUARTERLY, 2ND	USPQ2D
UNITED STATES REPORTS	US
U.S. CIRCUIT COURT REPORTS (D.C. CIR)	APPDC
U.S. CLAIMS COURT REPORTER	CLCT
U.S. COURT OF CLAIMS REPORTS	CTCL
U.S. COURT OF CUSTOM & PATENT APPEALS REPORTS (CUSTOMS)	CCPA
U.S. COURT OF CUSTOM & PATENT APPEALS REPORTS (PATENTS)	CCPA
U.S. COURT OF CUSTOMS APPEALS REPORTS	CTCUSTAPP
U.S. COURT OF INTERNATIONAL TRADE REPORTS	CIT
U.S. SUPREME COURT APPENDIX CASES	USAPPX
U.S. SUPREME COURT REPORTER	SCT
U.S. SUPREME COURT REPORTS, LAWYER'S ED.	LED
U.S. SUPREME COURT REPORTS, LAWYER'S ED., 2ND	LED2D
U.S. TAX CASES	USTC
U.S. TAX COURT MEMORANDUM DECISIONS	TCM
U.S. TAX COURT MEMORANDUM DECISIONS (BY NUMBER)	TCMEMO
UTAH REPORTS	UTAH
UTAH REPORTS, 2ND	UTAH2D
UTAH ADVANCE REPORTS	UTAHADVREP
VERMONT REPORTS	VT
VIRGINIA REPORTS	VA

(*continued*)

REPORTER	AUTO-CITE ABBREVIATION
VIRGINIA COURT OF APPEALS (REPORTS OF CASES DECIDED IN THE COURT OF APPEALS OF VIRGINIA)	VAAPP
VIRGINIA DECISIONS	VADEC
VIRGINIA LAW REPORTS	VLR
WAGES AND HOURS CASES (BNA)	WH
WALKER'S PENNSYLVANIA REPORTS	WALK
WALKER'S MICHIGAN CHANCERY REPORTS	WALKCH
WASHINGTON REPORTS	WASH
WASHINGTON REPORTS, 2ND	WASH2D
WASHINGTON COURT OF APPEALS REPORTS	WASHAPP
WASHINGTON TERRITORY REPORTS	WASHTERR
WATTS' REPORTS (PA)	WATTS
WATTS & SERGEANT REPORTS (PA)	WATTS&S
WEST VIRGINIA REPORTS	WVA
WHARTON'S REPORTS (PA)	WHART
WISCONSIN REPORTS	WIS
WISCONSIN REPORTS, 2ND	WIS2D
WYOMING REPORTS	WYO
WYTHE'S CHANCERY REPORTS (VA)	WHTHECH
YEATES' REPORTS (PA)	YEATES

INDEX